The Real Jesus

A DEVOTIONAL

by Jen Bradbury

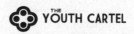

THE
YOUTH CARTEL

The Real Jesus: A Devotional

Copyright © 2016 by Jen Bradbury

Publisher: Mark Oestreicher
Managing Editor: Tamara Rice
Cover Design: Adam McLane
Layout: Marilee Pankratz
Creative Director: Superstar

All rights reserved. No part of this book may be reproduced in any form
by any electronic or mechanical means including photocopying,
recording, or information storage and retrieval without permission
in writing from the author.

All Scripture quotations, unless otherwise indicated, are taken from the Holy
Bible, New International Version®, NIV®. Copyright ©1973, 1978, 1984, 2011 by
Biblica, Inc.™ Used by permission of Zondervan. All rights reserved worldwide.
www.zondervan.com The "NIV" and "New International Version" are trademarks
registered in the United States Patent and Trademark Office by Biblica, Inc.™

Scripture marked NKJV from the New King James Version. Copyright © 1982
by Thomas Nelson, Inc. Used by permission. All rights reserved.

Scripture marked BSB from the Berean Study Bible. Copyright © 2016
by Bible Hub and Berean.Bible. Used by permission. All rights reserved.

Scripture marked NRSVA from the New Revised Standard Version Bible:
Anglicised Edition, copyright © 1989, 1995 the Division of Christian Education of
the National Council of the Churches of Christ in the United States of America.
Used by permission. All rights reserved.

Scripture marked ISV from the Holy Bible: International Standard Version®.
Copyright © 1996-forever by The ISV Foundation. ALL RIGHTS RESERVED
INTERNATIONALLY. Used by permission.

Scripture marked ESV are from the ESV® Bible (The Holy Bible, English Standard
Version®), copyright © 2001 by Crossway, a publishing ministry of Good News
Publishers. Used by permission. All rights reserved.

ISBN-13: 978-1-942145-19-6
ISBN-10: 1-942145-19-5

The Youth Cartel, LLC
www.theyouthcartel.com
Email: info@theyouthcartel.com
Born in San Diego
Printed in the U.S.A.

To Hope.
May you know and love Jesus;
May you follow Jesus wherever he leads;
And may you come to understand that Jesus is your hope.

CONTENTS

A Note to Youth Workers and Parents

Prompted by an assignment for grad school, I interviewed teens in my youth ministry in order to better understand what they believed about Jesus. I was stunned and perhaps more accurately, horrified to discover how little my teens knew about Jesus—the person on whom all of Christianity is based. Wanting to know if this phenomenon was more widespread than my own youth ministry, I embarked on a year-long research project to learn what other teens believed about Jesus. During this research project, I surveyed teens from throughout the country and visited four representative congregations in order to talk with teens, youth workers, and parents about their beliefs about Jesus. You can read more about the results from this study in *The Jesus Gap*, but suffice it to say, the Christology (beliefs about Jesus) of teens is poor. Many church teens don't acknowledge that Jesus is God or even a necessary part of our Christian faith.

The book you're now holding flows directly from my research, exploring the most pressing gaps I found in what teens believe about Jesus. It examines who Jesus is, Jesus' divinity and sinlessness, the ways in which Jesus was and is like us, what Jesus did and taught, why Jesus died, the necessity of Jesus to the Christian faith, and the difference Jesus makes in people's lives.

There's no right or wrong way to use this book. You can put it in the hands of teens and challenge them to use it as a daily devotional or to read it in one fell swoop. You could use this book in a small group environment, reading and discussing a few chapters each week. Youth workers could also use it as a roadmap for a teaching series about Jesus.

Each chapter contains real quotes from actual teenagers I interviewed—sometimes what they say about Jesus is orthodox, sometimes it's not. The quotes are not there to be instructive, but to spark reflection and deeper thinking.

Each chapter also contains a series of questions called Jesus Talk. These questions can be used as journal prompts for teens to continue thinking about this material on their own or as discussion questions for groups. However you choose to use them, challenging teens to actually think about and discuss their answers to these questions is important. You see, one of the findings from my research is that the more teens talk specifically about Jesus, the better their understanding of him actually is.

Regardless of how you choose to use this book, I'd encourage you to discuss **Section 7: Why Did Jesus Die?** with teens. This section explores multiple ways of answering the question. Even though you may (actually, I can almost guarantee you will!) disagree with at least some of these atonement theories, my research found it's helpful for teens to at least consider the different beliefs about Jesus that exist within Christendom. Here's why.

Our own answer to these important questions may not make sense to teens. Consider one teen I interviewed as part of my research. When I asked her, "Why did Jesus die?" she immediately responded with, "Jesus died for my sins." She then sat in silence for a moment before continuing, "At least that's what I've always been told. But I don't get it. How can the death of *one* man make up for *my* sins? I mean, he didn't commit those sins. I did. I just think there's gotta be more to this." While the substitutionary atonement theory she'd always been taught failed to make sense to this girl, other atonement theories (also rooted in Scripture) did. They gave her the language to articulate for herself why Jesus died, an important element in taking ownership of her faith.

At some point, our teens will meet other Christians whose beliefs about things like why Jesus died may differ from their own (or from what they've been taught to believe). Imagine, for example, how confusing it might be for someone who's grown up hearing only about the ransom theory of atonement to suddenly find himself in a congregation that talks about Jesus' death only using language from the substitutionary theory of atonement, something the pastor says is the right way of understanding Jesus' death. Being told his beliefs are *wrong* by other Christians might cause this young person to disregard the entirety of his faith—unless, of course, he's already been taught about the diverse ways in which Christians understand Jesus' death and decided for himself what he believes.

When teens decide for themselves what they believe, their faith in Jesus is strengthened. Far from weakening their faith, learning about beliefs that contradict their own causes teens to think deeply. When teens know what they believe about Jesus and why they believe it, they're far more likely to continue following him after they graduate from our youth ministries and begin to face real-life challenges.

I wholeheartedly believe that the better we know a person, the more deeply we can love him. The same, I think, is true of our relationship with Jesus. My hope is that this book will be a valuable tool you can use to help your teens get to know Jesus better so that they, too, can fall more deeply in love with him. As teens fall more deeply in love with Jesus and better understand who he was, what he did, and why it matters in their lives both now and in the future, I'm convinced that our ministries—and world—will never be the same.

A Note to Teens

Jesus: He's the center of our Christian faith. He's also controversial and utterly confusing.

When it comes to Jesus, the topics covered in this book are some of the most confusing ones out there. I know this because teens told me they were. You see, I spent nearly a year talking to hundreds of teens like you in order to learn what they believed about Jesus.

You'll meet some of these teens in the sidebar quotes found in each chapter in this book. While people's names have been changed, these quotes are real; they're what actual high school teens who are active in their church's youth ministry told me about Jesus. Some of these quotes might mirror your own thoughts about Jesus, but then again, some might not. That's okay.

While I agree with some of the quotes, I don't agree with all of them. *In fact, some of these quotes are in direct opposition to what this book suggests about Jesus.* But because they're what real teens actually believe about Jesus, they're important. While the quotes themselves haven't been changed, the names of those who said them have been.

My hope is that this book—and the quotes from teenagers found within it—will challenge you to think deeply about Jesus and decide for yourself how to answer the question Jesus asks his friend Peter: "Who do you say that I am?"

—Jen

Section One

Will the Real JESUS Please Stand Up?

"I like to think of Jesus as a fun person to be around. The Bible always talks about the serious things. Jesus probably had a good sense of humor. What person would be followed if he wasn't fun or didn't have a good sense of humor?"
— JORDAN

1: Who Is JESUS?

The first time my husband, Doug, and I met, we were seniors in high school, both attending a student introduction to engineering weekend at the University of Illinois. We were assigned to the same bridge-building group. After our weekend-long encounter, I knew that Doug was an engineering major.

The next fall, I ran into Doug again on my dorm floor. He was there visiting a girl he knew from high school. He thought they were friends. She thought they were still dating. From this, I learned Doug wasn't great at ending relationships.

The next time I encountered Doug it was in Physics 111, where we were in the same discussion group. Here, I learned Doug was crazy smart and also a great teacher. I passed physics because of his help.

Shortly thereafter, Doug invited me to attend a worship service at his campus ministry. This is how I learned Doug loved Jesus.

Each of these encounters with Doug taught me something different about him. Alone, none of these instances taught me everything there was to know about Doug. Isolate any one of them from the others and you get a very incomplete picture of him. Actually, even when you combine all of these things together in a list, your picture of Doug is still pretty incomplete. You know a few things about him that might lead you to draw some conclusions about him, some of which could be right but a lot of which would probably be untrue. For better or worse, our individual snapshots of a person become the entire basis for how we see him or her. The snapshots form an image that shapes our understanding and determines whether or not we like the person.

We do the same thing with Jesus. Each of us have snapshots of him.

"Jesus is the son of God. He came to this earth to teach us how to live and he will come again to judge us."
- TIM

There's angelic Baby Jesus.

There's the Nice Jesus we learned about in Sunday school, who we'll be talking about later in this section along with Superhero Jesus and Spiritual Guru Jesus.

There's the Homeboy Jesus we see on t-shirts.

There's Hipster Jesus with the long hair.

There's White Jesus... And Black Jesus... And Asian Jesus.

There's Bloody Jesus on the cross and the Resurrected Jesus who, like a ghost, passes through doors and walls.

There's Jesus the Revolutionist... And Jesus the Pacifist.

There's Jesus, the guy who's powerful enough to perform miracles and fix everything... And there's also Jesus, the guy who gets frustrated by how many people want his help.

There's Jesus, the guy from Nazareth... And there's Jesus, the God from heaven.

These snapshots of Jesus aren't necessarily wrong... but they are incomplete. And that can become problematic, because sometimes, rather than combining these different snapshots to form a more complete picture of Jesus, we instead choose one as the basis for our entire understanding of him. When we do, Jesus becomes pretty one-dimensional; he becomes simple rather than the complex person he was and is. This can cause us to miss something important about him—something that might just change our understanding of him and our faith.

It's like with Doug. If I'd based my understanding of him solely on the fact that he was an engineering major, I might have concluded that even though he was smart, he was socially awkward, unable to really talk to people (something that Doug actually does quite well).

Or if I'd based my understanding of him solely on his former girlfriend's impression of him (the one who thought she was still dating him), I might have concluded that Doug wasn't good boyfriend—let alone good husband—material. I might have missed how caring Doug is, how he's willing to do anything for those he loves.

"Jesus is the Messiah, someone who tried to end wrongdoings in religion."
- CHRISTY

My husband can't be reduced to a list of facts about him.

Neither can Jesus.

In some ways, the better we get to know Jesus, the more mysterious he becomes. At the same time, the more we get to know Jesus, the better we understand him and the more clear it becomes that he is both fully God and fully human, both Savior and friend. The better we get to know Jesus, the more it becomes clear that no one snapshot can accurately portray him.

Jesus is so much more than that.

JESUS Talk

1. Jen mentions several common snapshots of Jesus. What other snapshots of Jesus would you have included in her list? How have these snapshots impacted your understanding of Jesus?
2. Of the snapshots of Jesus that Jen lists, which have most influenced your understanding of him? Why?
3. Why might it be problematic to our faith to focus on only snapshot of Jesus?
4. How can Jesus be both fully God and fully human? Both savior and friend?
5. How would you answer the question that is the title of this chapter, "Who is Jesus?"

"I've pictured Jesus being strong. He could do anything. He could help people lift things they can't lift."

— APRIL

2: JESUS: More than Superman

There's been a lot of superhero movies lately: *The Avengers, Thor, Captain America, The Amazing Spider-Man, Batman,* and *Man of Steel.*

Of all of them, *Man of Steel* is my favorite, perhaps because I get a little nostalgic when it comes to Superman. I grew up watching the old Superman movies, the ones starring Christopher Reeves. In junior high and high school, my family spent Sunday nights watching *Lois and Clark: The New Adventures of Superman.*

In some ways, I feel like I've watched the evolution of Superman. Even so, no matter which version of Superman I've seen, one thing has consistently remained the same: Like every superhero, Superman has an alter ego—Clark Kent—who lives an entirely normal life. It's the ordinariness of Clark Kent that makes Superman likable. It's also what makes it possible for us to relate to Superman. Without Clark Kent, Superman would be so different from us that it'd be impossible for us to relate to him. I mean, I can barely lift a 20 lb. bag of cat litter. There's no way I could lift an entire offshore oil well and keep it from falling into a fire the way Superman does at the start of *Man of Steel.* And for me to get around Chicago, I have to navigate grueling traffic. As much as I want to, I can't fly overhead like Superman does.

It's the existence of an alter ego that I think makes it easy to compare

Jesus to a superhero. On the one hand, we've got Jesus of Nazareth—an ordinary carpenter from the wrong side of the tracks. On the other hand, we've got Jesus the Christ—the God who performs superhuman stunts like walking on water and raising people from the dead. Maybe that's why every time a superhero movie releases, it's followed by a wave of churches doing "superhero" sermon series.

In some ways, I get that. There's some truth to the Superhero Jesus comparison.

Like Superman, Superhero Jesus is not of this world. He's otherworldly. Even though he was born on earth, his dad—God—wasn't.

Like Superman, Superhero Jesus has got supernatural powers, including the ability to perform miracles. Just as Superman must choose to use his powers to benefit the world, so must Jesus.

"Jesus is a being that is human and non-human."

— CHRIS

Just as Superman has a nemesis in Lex Luther, Jesus has one in Satan, who he courageously fights in order to free the world from darkness.

Just as Superman is willing to sacrifice himself to save others, so too, is Superhero Jesus. Despite the cross, death cannot actually defeat Superhero Jesus, who emerges victorious.

Certainly, there's some aspects of Superhero Jesus that are accurate. God really did send Jesus to save us. But unlike superheroes who are often created or sent to earth by accident, God sent Jesus to earth intentionally. Jesus also had supernatural powers that allowed him to perform miracles—including the greatest one of all: His resurrection. Through Jesus' resurrection, death and evil have been defeated.

But here's the thing: There are some problems with thinking about Jesus as a superhero.

For one, superheroes have a tendency to disappear—just ask Lois Lane. So even though we believe that in a time of crisis Superhero Jesus will show up and conquer our enemies, we're unsure if he'll stay when the crisis is over. Our hope in Superhero Jesus wanes whenever we confront small problems—the kind we convince ourselves superheroes don't have time for.

In actuality, the real Jesus is always with us. In fact, some of Jesus' last words to his followers were, "Surely I am with you always to the very end of the age" (Matthew 28:20).

Jesus is with us—in times of great crisis, yes, but also when we face small problems. Beyond that, Jesus is with us during life's ordinary moments, the times when things are actually going pretty well.

Another problem with comparing Jesus to a superhero is that superheroes all have a fatal flaw—just ask Superman how much he loves kryptonite. So when we think of Jesus as a superhero, we mistakenly believe he does too. We start to think that something can eventually undo him—that he is, in some way, imperfect.

But Jesus was and is perfect. He's without sin. Unlike Superman, Jesus has no kryptonite. He'll never grow weak or weary. We need not fear that eventually he'll let his guard down so much that the world will be threatened in another sequel: *SuperJesus Part IV*.

"Jesus is humanity's last hope, who died for us out of unconditional love."

— GRANT

In fact, Jesus promises us the opposite: That through him the world—and everything in it—will actually be made new. That brings us to a really important difference between Jesus and superheroes, perhaps the most important difference of all. Superheroes always risk their lives, but they never actually give them up. Just when we think they're dead, they step out of the rubble. In contrast, Jesus actually died. But through his death on the cross, he won. And so did we.

So yes, in some ways Jesus is like a superhero. But even your favorite superhero is only a fraction of who Jesus is... Only a fraction as powerful, a fraction as kind, a fraction as good, a fraction as just.

Unlike any superhero I've ever heard of, Jesus is the ultimate everything—to whom no one else can even begin to compare.

JESUS Talk

1. How is Jesus like a superhero?
2. How is Jesus different than a superhero?
3. How might thinking about Jesus as a superhero be helpful to your faith? How might it be harmful?
4. When have you encountered Jesus during one of life's ordinary moments?
5. In light of this chapter, how would you answer the question, "Who is Jesus?"

"Jesus takes a somewhat wimpy lifestyle and embraces it to make it bold and strong."

— NATTIE

3: JESUS: More than a Nice Guy

I grew up in a house without cable TV. This meant that as a young child, there were very few TV shows my parents let me watch. The exception was whatever was on PBS—usually *Sesame Street* or *Mister Rodgers' Neighborhood*. What I remember about Mr. Rodgers can be summed up in three words: He was nice.

Mr. Rodgers spoke in soft tones, wore a sweater, and always appeared super gentle. He taught me—and many other kids—to be kind to our neighbor, perpetually asking us, "Won't you be my neighbor?"

It seems pretty obvious to me now that Mr. Rodgers—a Presbyterian minister—borrowed a lot of his best stuff, including the whole neighbor thing, from Jesus. Long before Mr. Rodgers taught us to be kind to our neighbor, Jesus taught us to show our neighbor mercy.

In the parable of the Good Samaritan, Jesus tells the story of a man who's walking from Jerusalem to Jericho. Along the way, some robbers beat him up, leaving him naked and half dead. Shortly thereafter, a priest comes along. Rather than help the man, the priest crosses to the other side of the road and continues on his way. So, too, does a Levite, someone else who worked in the temple. Thankfully, a third person comes along. This guy's a Samaritan— from a group of people whom the Jews despised.

Yet, it's this guy—the Samaritan—who takes time out of his busy schedule to help the half-dead man. He bandages him, puts him on his donkey, and takes him to the nearest hotel. There, he stays with the man overnight, caring for him. In the morning, he pays the bill and even gives the hotel owner extra money so that he can keep looking after the half-dead man.

According to Jesus, it's this last man—the Samaritan—who's the only one who actually behaves like a neighbor to the half-dead man. It's this Samaritan who shows him mercy, despite their different ethnicities (Luke 10:30-37).

Through stories like this one, Jesus teaches his followers to be kind and compassionate to one another. Elsewhere, he explicitly tells his followers to "love one another" (John 13:34).

For this reason, when we picture Jesus, we often picture someone who's a lot like Mr. Rodgers: just plain nice. We might even call this version of Jesus *Nice Jesus*.

Like Mr. Rodgers, Nice Jesus is someone who's easy to like. Unfortunately though, Nice Jesus isn't super helpful. Like Mr. Rodgers, he can teach us to be kind and compassionate—to be nice to others—but he can't really do anything about it when we're not. Mr. Rodgers is just too nice for that. So is Nice Jesus.

"In the garden before his crucifixion, it is a little wimpy that he begs not to die when he knew it was coming all along."

— SANDRA

After all, Jesus told people, "Love your enemies and pray for those who persecute you" and "I tell you, do not resist an evil person. If anyone slaps you on the right cheek, turn to them the other cheek also" (Matthew 5:44, 39).

You know what we call people like that today?

Wimps.

I don't know about you, but I don't want to worship a wimp. It doesn't matter how nice he is.

Why?

Because wimps aren't worthy of our worship.

Wimps might be good, but they aren't necessarily strong. They're certainly not powerful. They fade into the background. They're easy to run over and ignore because they have no backbone. Since they never want to offend or hurt anyone, they won't stand up for themselves or for those most in need of an advocate.

Similarly, nice guys are weak. Far from being the protector of others, they're the ones who need protecting. In the face of injustice, nice guys run inside and cower behind locked doors, too frightened by our scary world to do anything else. Rather than act, nice guys sit back and passively wait for change to come.

That's not what Jesus did; that's not who Jesus is.

Far from passively waiting for change to come, Jesus changes everyone he encounters. His love for people is active. He crosses barriers. He hangs out with the outcasts. He defends those who need protection. He's both a good neighbor and a good leader.

> "Jesus stands up for himself no matter the battle and gets it done without bloodshed. If some people say he doesn't fight so that makes him a wimp then they are wrong; he stands up and gets it done."
>
> — SAM

Jesus is nice and he's loving—so loving that he won't stand for injustice. He's nice and he's powerful—so powerful that he defeats death without shedding any blood other than his own.

Jesus is nice but he's no wimp. There's no one better to have in your corner.

Thankfully, he is.

JESUS Talk

1. Do you agree or disagree that Nice Jesus isn't super helpful? Why?
2. Have you ever felt like Jesus was a wimp? If so, when? What led you to that conclusion?
3. How might thinking about Jesus as a nice guy be helpful to your faith? How might it be harmful?
4. "Far from passively waiting for change to come, Jesus changes everyone he encounters." How has Jesus changed you?
5. In light of this chapter, how would you answer the question, "Who is Jesus?"

"Jesus is our role model. We should follow in his footsteps and look to him for guidance."

— AMIE

4: JESUS: More than a Spiritual Guru

I'm not Catholic, but I went to a Catholic high school.

I still remember the first time my high school offered confession.

In the Catholic tradition, confession is a big deal. In fact, it's considered a sacrament, a way of experiencing God's grace.

During confession, you meet with a priest. Sometimes you do so face to face but more often than not, you're separated from the priest by a wall or curtain in order to protect your identity. That way, you can be honest about your sins without fear of someone judging you.

At the start of confession, the priest asks you how long it's been since your last confession. After telling him, you then list the ways you've sinned since then. After confessing your sins, the priest gives you something to do—like say five rosaries and three Hail Mary's—as punishment for your sin. He then tells you your sins are forgiven.

To be honest, this kind of confession terrified me—especially since I didn't understand why I needed to confess my sins to a priest in the first place. I wondered, "What made a priest any better than me? Why could he listen to and forgive my sins when he was also a sinner, just like me?"

Part of my confusion lay in the fact that I equated Catholic priests with the pastors in my own protestant congregation, and I couldn't imagine doing this type of confession with them. I mean, I called my pastors by their first names. I'd been in their homes, hung out with their families, and laughed with them. They seemed so ordinary to me.

What I learned from my Catholic friends is they didn't quite see their priests like I did. Priests were different than them. They couldn't get married. They had no kids. Many lived not in ordinary houses, but in homes attached to their parishes. They wore black pants and shirts with clerical collars, which they covered with white robes adorned with fancy stoles and hoods. Their priorities were simply church and God.

To my Catholic friends, priests were a special category of people, whose training and lifestyle connected them to God in a way that ordinary people did not experience. For this reason, it made sense to my friends to confess their sins to their priests, who could then offer them forgiveness on behalf of God.

Catholic or not, sometimes we view Jesus in the same way. We see him as a good person with a special connection to God: A spiritual guru, if you will. Let's call this version of Jesus *Spiritual Guru Jesus*.

This special connection allows Spiritual Guru Jesus to do some pretty incredible things like forgive people's sins and even perform miracles. It also gives him a lot of spiritual knowledge and an extra dose of holiness. There's something *almost* otherworldly about him.

"Jesus was the son of God, God's right-hand man."

— JUSTIN

But, you see, the key word here is *almost*.

Spiritual Guru Jesus is *almost otherworldly*, but he's not actually otherworldly.

Spiritual Guru Jesus has a special connection with God, but he's not actually God.

As a result, there are some problems with Spiritual Guru Jesus. Since he's not God himself, ultimately Spiritual Guru Jesus can't do anything more than provide us with the type of counseling and advice we might get from a good pastor, priest, or counselor. He can offer us forgiveness on behalf of God, but he can't actually forgive us himself.

In actuality, Jesus doesn't offer us forgiveness on behalf of God. He forgives us because he *is* God. That's what the author of Hebrews means when he writes, "Such a high priest truly meets our need—one who is holy, blameless, pure, set apart from sinners, exalted above the heavens. Unlike the other high priests, he does not need to offer sacrifices day after day, first for his own sins, and then for the sins of the people. He sacrificed for their sins once for all when he offered himself" (Hebrews 7:26-27).

What priests do when they offer people forgiveness isn't wrong. But it isn't exactly complete either. It can't be since they're not God.

"Jesus is a mentor who you go to when you are lost and need guidance."
— STEVE

In contrast, when Jesus offers us forgiveness, it's complete. Nothing else needs to happen. No one else needs to forgive us. That's because in Jesus, we get more than a Spiritual Guru who connects us to God.

We get God himself.

JESUS Talk

1. How, if at all, does your congregation practice confession?
2. What's the difference between the forgiveness you receive from a priest or pastor and the forgiveness you receive from Jesus?
3. How might thinking about Jesus as a spiritual guru be helpful to your faith? How might it be harmful?
4. In light of this chapter, how would you answer the question, "Who is Jesus?"

5: **JESUS:** Better than a Bestie

In high school, I had different friends for different occasions. Here's what I mean.

I had church friends who I did the God thing with. They called me Jenny.

I had work friends who were a part of my life from 3:00-6:00 p.m. on weekdays when I worked at the bagel shop. They called me Jennifer.

I had school friends who I studied and chatted with between classes. They called me Jen.

I had friends who I met through extracurricular activities. We shared common interests and passions. They also called me Jen.

Because my life was so fragmented, I often felt incomplete around my various groups of friends—like I couldn't quite be the same person around all of them. I mean, would my work friends who swore constantly still like me if they knew how important my faith was to me? Would my church friends still like me if they knew how smart I was? Would my school friends like me if I stopped helping them with calculus? Would my yearbook friends like me if they knew I liked science as much as writing?

In the midst of my fragmented life, I attended a retreat with my high school youth group during which we discussed friendships. As part of this, we put our arms around each other and belted out the words to Christian singer Michael W. Smith's song "Friends":

And friends are friends forever
If the Lord's the Lord of them
And a friend will not say never
'Cause the welcome will not end

Though it's hard to let you go
In the Father's hands we know
That a lifetime's not too long
To live as friends

Even though I belted those words out along with everyone else, inside I was skeptical. Was it really possible to be lifelong friends with someone? What's more, did I even want to be? Only being able to share select parts of myself with people was becoming increasingly frustrating.

It was at that same retreat when I was first told Jesus was my friend. To be honest, this sounded incredibly weird to me. If I couldn't see Jesus, how could we be friends? Wouldn't being friends with an invisible Jesus make me seem crazy—like an adult who still has an imaginary friend?

Despite this, I opened my Bible to the passage we were discussing: John 15:15-16. Here, Jesus tells his disciples, "I no longer call you servants, because a servant does not know his master's business. Instead, I have called you friends, for everything that I learned from my Father I have made known to you. You did not choose me, but I chose you and appointed you to go and bear fruit—fruit that will last."

It sure sounds like Jesus wants to be our friend. I mean, he CHOSE us.

Still, I couldn't help but wonder: Which *part* of me did he choose? Who'd he want to be friends with? Church Jenny? Work Jennifer? School Jen?

At the time, I didn't dare share my questions. I feared doing so would make people judge me. So I kept my mouth shut. But that passage stuck with me.

When I reflect back on that passage now, here's what I've realized: My sophomore self was projecting my human experience on Jesus. Because my friendships were so fragmented, I assumed a friendship with Jesus would also be fragmented. I created Jesus in my own image... or at least in the image of my friends. I don't think that was Jesus' intent in this passage.

In actuality, I think Jesus was saying something really remarkable. You see, up until this point, God was always distant from his people. That makes sense. We can't see God the Father, who has no body. What's more, the Jews believed God's name was so sacred, so holy, they refused to even utter it.

It's hard to be friends with someone whose name you can't even say.

But Jesus bridges the gap between God the Father and us. In John 15:15-16, it's like he's saying, "You and me, we're friends. Of course you can call me by name."

In Jesus, God becomes touchable—so much so that it actually becomes possible to enter into a friendship with God, the Creator of the universe.

How crazy is that?

Jesus is someone we can hang out with, laugh with, and have fun with. He's relatable and present in our lives. Unlike some of our friends, when the going gets tough, Jesus doesn't leave. He stays.

Jesus also isn't afraid of conflict. Jesus loves us so much that he tells us the truth—even when it's hard for us to hear. He even wants to hear our truth. He's not afraid of pain, nor is he afraid of tears. Jesus is tough, so tough that our friendship with him can weather hard things. What's more, unlike all our other friends, Jesus can do more than just sit with us in the storms of life, he can actually calm them. Perhaps most remarkably though, Jesus loves our whole selves.

"Jesus is my homie."

— MIA

Jesus doesn't just want to be friends with one part of you; he wants to be friends with your entire being. He wants to know the REAL you—even if you're still not sure who that is. Because Jesus knows the real you, the complete you, his love for you is also complete. Jesus is a friend like no other.

No matter how awesome your best friend is, Jesus is better.

No matter how long you've known your best friend, Jesus has known you longer. He knew you while you were still in the womb... and he'll know you until the day you die.

For that reason, in Jesus, we really do have someone who will be our friend forever.

JESUS Talk

1. What different friend groups are you a part of?
2. In what ways do you create Jesus in your own image or that of your friends?
3. What does it mean to you that "Jesus wants to be friends with your entire being"?
4. "No matter how awesome your best friend is, Jesus is better." Why?
5. How might thinking about Jesus as a friend be helpful to your faith? How might it be harmful?
6. In light of this chapter, how would you answer the question, "Who is Jesus?"

"Jesus was born into the world as a king, but he wasn't born into a royal family. That's very significant because Jesus did not have the 'credentials' for people to worship him as a king. People didn't worship him because they had to, they worshiped him because they wanted to."

— SARAH

6: King JESUS

I've been fortunate enough to visit England twice. Both times, I've gone to Buckingham Palace and watched the changing of the guard. Both times, I've thought, "How can people who live like this relate to commoners like me?"

That said, I'll admit I'm fascinated by the royals. I search the royals section of People.com a little too frequently. My favorite pastime as I wait in line at the grocery store is scanning the tabloid headlines to see what's new with Prince William, Princess Kate, and even Prince Harry.

Part of my fascination with the royals is, I think, that I don't entirely understand the point of them. What do they do? Why does England have both a royal family and a prime minister?

Since I don't entirely understand the point of having a king or a queen, it's sometimes hard for me to think about Jesus as a king. But whether I like it or not, the Bible certainly describes Jesus as one, starting when he's a baby and Magi come to worship and bring him gifts (Matthew 2:1-12).

Once he begins his public ministry, Jesus talks frequently about the Kingdom of God. Where there's a kingdom, there's got to be a king—someone who rules over the kingdom with authority and power.

Now, if you're like me, that might make you a little nervous. I sure as heck don't want anyone ruling over me. After all, I'm an independent person with rights. What's more, I know that kings and queens don't always have the best track records. Consider these examples from England:

King Henry VIII murdered two of his wives for failing to provide him with a son.

Queen Mary I attempted to return England to Catholicism. To make her point, she burned 285 Protestants at the stake and earned the nickname "Bloody Mary."

Mary Queen of Scots was a suspect in multiple murders (including her husband's). She was also a suspect in numerous plots to assassinate the English queen, which eventually led to a trial for treason and to her execution.

Then there are the kings and queens who simply mismanaged their country, led them into unnecessary or failed wars, or slept around.

Clearly, kings and queens do not always put the needs of their citizens ahead of their own. More often than not, power corrupts them. Given this, if Jesus is our king, will power one day corrupt him? Will he eventually look out for his own interests more than ours?

To answer these questions, consider the evidence.

In Mark 8:29, Jesus asks his friend and apostle Peter, "Who do you say I am?" Peter answers by saying, "You are the Christ."

Today, we often use the word *Christ* as kind of a last name for Jesus. In actuality, *Christ* means "anointed one." In Jesus' time, kings were typically anointed at a kind of coronation. Usually, the person anointing them was a well-respected, older male.

Jesus, however, experiences a different kind of anointing. According to Jesus' friend and apostle Matthew, Jesus is anointed while visiting Simon the Leper in Bethany. There, a "sinful" woman comes up to him with an alabaster jar of very expensive perfume and pours it over his head (Matthew 26:6-7).

"Jesus cares about the good of his people rather than riches and luxuries."

— JOSH

This would have been unheard of in Jesus' time. No king would have had a woman do his anointing, especially not one described as "sinful" (Luke 7:37). To do so would have made him appear weak, not powerful. Yet, it's a sinful woman who anoints King Jesus— an unusual anointing for an unusual king. Can such a king be corrupted?

In case you're still not convinced, let's return to Peter's declaration that Jesus is the Christ, the anointed one. When Peter calls Jesus the Christ, Jesus doesn't dispute him. He does, however, immediately tell his apostles that the "Son of Man must suffer many things, and be rejected by the elders, chief priests, and teachers of the law, and that he must be killed and after three days rise again" (Mark 8:31).

Do you see anything strange about this?

I do.

Most people with a lot of power assume they're invincible, that they're going to live forever. They think their power will protect them from suffering—not cause it.

That's not the case with Jesus, who pretty much accepts the title of King and then in the same breath says not just that he's going to suffer, but that he *must* suffer. By saying these strange things, Jesus is essentially telling his friends, "Yep. I'm your King. I'm the King to end all kings. But I'm a very different kind of king."

Can power really corrupt a king who's willing to suffer?

Just in case you still think the answer to this question is *yes*, take a look at another example of the kind of king Jesus is going to be. In Mark 11:1-10, Jesus rides into Jerusalem to a cheering crowd. I imagine this scene would have looked a little like the hometown parades *American Idol* gives their final three contestants each year, with fans eagerly lining the roads and cheering, hoping to catch a glimpse of their idol—their king or queen.

In Jesus' day, these kinds of parades were common for kings, who'd ride in on a powerful war horse as people bowed down to worship them.

There's one notable difference about Jesus' parade. He enters Jerusalem not on a powerful war horse but a scrawny donkey.

If you've never seen a donkey, let me tell you there's nothing impressive about them. They're incredibly ornery. They'd never be used in war because they act out too much. They can't be trained the way a horse can. Far from arriving amidst pomp and circumstance, Jesus' entrance on such an animal would have likely been far more circus-like. It would have been humbling to say the least.

Once again, by participating in something typically reserved for a king, Jesus is acknowledging that he is indeed King. Yet, he does so with a twist, as if to say that while he's King, he's a different kind of king—one who is humble, not arrogant.

Do we really need to worry that such a humble king will one day turn selfish?

Again, just in case you're still tempted to answer *yes*, consider one final example from Jesus' life.

Not only does King Jesus talk about suffering, he actually dies on the cross. A sign is placed above him that reads, "This is Jesus, the

King of the Jews" (Matthew 27:37).

To be sure, lots of kings have died during their reigns. But unlike Jesus, none of them did so willingly—especially not if they had the power to stop their deaths from happening like Jesus did.

When Peter pulls out a sword and tries to defend him during his arrest, Jesus responds, saying, "Do you think I cannot call on my Father, and he will at once put at my disposal more than twelve legions of angels?" (Matthew 26:53).

In the moments leading up to his death, Jesus is not powerless. He simply chooses not to use his power so that he can do his Father's will. He dies willingly, for you and for me.

A king who's willing to die for us seems like one who's unlikely to put his own needs before ours.

Beyond that, a king who's anointed by a sinful woman, who rides in on a donkey rather than a war horse, and who willingly suffers and dies isn't only a different kind of king, he's the kind of king who combines majesty with humility, and justice with grace.

"Jesus is king in my life."

— CAITLYN

He's the kind of king who's truly worthy of our worship.

He's the only kind of king I'll follow.

Will you?

JESUS Talk

1. Has it ever made you nervous to think of Jesus as a king, with the power and authority to rule over you? Why or why not?
2. How is Jesus a different kind of king than the ones our world is used to?
3. Do you think power could ever corrupt King Jesus? Why or why not?
4. How willing are you to follow King Jesus? Why?
5. How might thinking about Jesus as a king be helpful to your faith? How might it be harmful?
6. In light of this chapter, how would you answer the question Jesus asks Peter, "Who do you say I am?"

Section Two

JESUS: God or Human?

"There's God the Father, God the Son, and God the Holy Spirit. There are three persons. They are coexisting. It's not just the son is little and God the father is big."

— JACQUELINE

7: JESUS: God's Mini-Me

One of the most confusing labels we give Jesus is that of God's Son.

I think when we say this we mean that Jesus is really God Jr.—God's mini-me who is somehow a little less important, a little less powerful than God the Father. But is that really what it means to say Jesus is God's Son?

To find out, let's look at one of the places in Scripture where Jesus is called God's Son: his baptism. This story happens at the start of Jesus' public ministry, when he goes out and finds his cousin, John the Baptist—someone who, at the time, was actually more widely known and recognized than Jesus.

Despite the fact that he's got more followers than Jesus, John knows his job is to prepare the way for Jesus, who he readily acknowledges is more powerful than him. Knowing this, initially John refuses Jesus' request to baptize him. Eventually, though, Jesus gets his way and John baptizes him.

At that moment, heaven is opened and the Spirit of God descends like a dove. All who are gathered there hear a voice from heaven saying, "This is my Son, whom I love, with him I am well pleased" (Matthew 3:16-17).

Now to us, God the Father's declaration might seem unimportant—

especially for those of us who have grown up in the church hearing
that Jesus is God's Son. But to the Jews watching Jesus' baptism, this
would have been an earth-shattering revelation. As Jews, the people
gathered at Jesus' baptism knew God the Father. They respected
him. They followed him. They even worshiped him.

But they didn't know Jesus. They had no reason to respect or
follow him, let alone worship him. Until, that is, they heard God
the Father—the one whom they respected—say loudly and clearly,
"This is my Son." Far from making Jesus less important, to those
gathered that day, his identity as God's Son is what would have
given him his authority and credibility.

To further enhance that credibility, God the Father gives Jesus an
extra endorsement. He reminds everyone that Jesus is loved and
that he has greatly pleased God. Essentially, God the Father tells
everyone, "I'm proud of my Son, Jesus, for his obedience and
faithfulness thus far and for what he's about to do."

God the Father's pride makes it clear that by reminding everyone
who Jesus is, he's not trying to put him in his place. He's affirming
him and reminding him of his authority. He's basically saying, "This
guy's with me. He's not less than me. He's *with* me. If you trust me,
you can trust him."

> It's almost as if Jesus is doing the dirty work for God. God makes all the
> decisions. He tells Jesus to go act them out. God himself could have come
> down to earth—instead he sent Jesus. Jesus is like his second in command."
>
> — ALLY

At Jesus' baptism, God the Father identifies him as part of his
family, along with the Holy Spirit, the third part of what we call the
Trinity. Each part of this family has a different job: God the Father
is our Creator. God the Son is our Savior. God the Holy Spirit is the
one who lives within us, who equips us for our work in the world.

Despite their different roles, each part of the Trinity is important. Each is fully God.

So yes, Jesus is God's Son. But that doesn't mean he's less than God the Father. It's simply a way of defining his relationship to God the Father—in the same way we might define our relationship to our parents.

For example, I once attended a large family reunion filled with people who, even though I was related to them, I'd never met. At that reunion, each of us wore a name tag containing our name (shocking, I know), as well as who we were related to. My name tag said: *Jen, daughter of Ron and Claudia Nelson.*

"Jesus is the son of God, who also was God."

— DAN

I quickly realized that at that family reunion, my name mattered little. What mattered far more was the fact that I was the daughter of Ron and Claudia Nelson. By identifying myself in terms of my relationship to my parents, my long-lost relatives could more easily figure out not only who I was, but how I was connected to our family. My relationship with my parents gave people a way of placing me. It helped them better understand me.

The same is true of Jesus.

Identifying Jesus as God's Son defines him relationally, it gives us a way of placing him and better understanding him. Just like I'm not less than Ron and Claudia because I'm their daughter, Jesus isn't less than God the Father because he's God's Son. He's his own person, always connected to God the Father, yet independent from him, proudly wearing a name tag that reads:

JESUS, SON OF GOD.

the real JESUS

JESUS Talk

1. How does knowing Jesus is God's Son give him authority and credibility?
2. Think about the three parts of the trinity. With which do you most relate? Why?
3. To you, what does it mean to say that Jesus is God's Son? Why?
4. Why does it matter to our faith that Jesus is God's Son?

"If we think about Jesus in biological terms, we realize that he was formed and born similar to us. However, thinking of him this way could also make it difficult to believe the fully-God and fully-human aspect."

— ME

8: Half and Half

As I write this, I'm 34 weeks pregnant. This means that physically, I'm huge. It also means that this baby of mine has been cooking for eight and a half months and that soon, my husband and I will get to meet her.

Now, at the risk of grossing you out, let's do a quick refresher on how babies are made.

Babies are made through sex.

More specifically, babies are made when a sperm (from a guy) fertilizes an egg (from a girl). Both the sperm and the egg contain DNA from the baby's parents and when they mix, you get a wonderful blend of both mom and dad. To put it another way, half of a baby's DNA comes from her mom and half of it comes from her dad. In essence, a baby is half and half.

With that in mind, think about Jesus.

According to Matthew 1:20, Jesus' biological dad was not Joseph but the Holy Spirit, aka, God. Jesus' mom was Mary, a human. So if Jesus got half his DNA from his dad and half from his mom, that makes him half and half, right? That makes Jesus half God and human, right?

Maybe according to biology, but not according to our faith.

Our faith says that even though Jesus was born as a baby, he was both fully God and fully human.

Now how can that be? Does such a belief require us to disregard the laws of science and in particular, biology?

NO.

You see, in the stories of creation told in Genesis, we meet God the Father as our Creator. Using only words, God the Father creates the entire world.

"Thinking about Jesus in biological terms bridges the gap between science and religion."

— SOPHIA

As our creator—as *the* Creator—God the Father knows how the world works and how people are created. What's more, he's actually the one who established the rules that govern how all things—including science—work. As the one who established the rules, God is above them. This makes it possible for God the Father—the Creator—to make Jesus both fully God *and* fully human.

Makes sense, right?

Well... kind of.

I mean, I can convince myself I'm satisfied by that answer, which I suppose on *some* level makes a little bit of sense.

Likewise, I can convince myself there are some things we just have to accept by faith. As the author of Hebrews says, "Faith is confidence in what we hope for and assurance about what we do not see" (Hebrews 11:1).

But if I'm honest, I'll admit that's hard for me to do. I'm guessing it might be hard for you to do as well.

So let me say this.

Through science, we know how babies are made. Even so, the first time I heard my baby girl's heartbeat on an ultrasound, I cried at this miraculous being growing inside of me. Even though I could tell you precisely how she was made from an egg and sperm meeting, I knew I was still witnessing a miracle.

That a baby forms from two lone cells is crazy. It sounds impossible.

Yet, science assures us that it's not.

> "We have to disregard the laws of biology to believe Jesus is fully God and fully human. Then again, a scientific law is defined as a statement based on repeated experimental observations. So really, a new observation could come into play and change it all (like Jesus)."
>
> — JENNY

What's more, science has also made it possible for me to know how large my baby has been throughout this pregnancy. For example: I knew going into my 12-week ultrasound that my baby was roughly two inches long (approximately the size of a lime.) Even so, I sat in awe as I watched my baby girl's very tiny, yet identifiable hands wave at me.

Through this pregnancy, I've learned that science and wonder can and do coexist, even today. In fact, I've even redefined science a bit. To me, science is the process of observing and trying to understand what God has made. Accordingly, there are some things—like babies—that can be explained by science and yet are still always miracles.

Maybe the same is true of Jesus.

Maybe biology only gets us so far. At some point, maybe we've just got to admit that like all babies, baby Jesus was a miracle. If that's the case, then maybe it's not such a stretch to believe he's also fully God and fully human.

I mean, biology may say it's impossible. But does that really matter when God, the Creator of all things including the rules of biology, is your dad?

JESUS Talk

1. How might it be helpful to your faith to think about Jesus in biological terms? Harmful to your faith?
2. Do you think that believing Jesus is fully God and fully human requires us to disregard the laws of biology? Why or why not?
3. What does it mean that "As the one who established the rules, God is above them"?
4. Jen defines science as "the process of observing and trying to understand what God has made." What would you add or delete from her definition? Why?
5. According to Jen, "There are some things—like babies—that can be explained by science and yet are still always miracles." Do you agree or disagree? Why? In addition to babies, what else is miraculous, despite the fact that it can be explained by science?
6. Why does it matter to our faith that Jesus was NOT half and half, but fully God and fully human?

"Jesus isn't just reflecting God's power; he HAS God's power because he is God. Without God's power and glory, he would just be a man or a prophet."

— JANICE

9: JESUS the Demigod?

Here's what I remember about mythology: I hated it. To this day, I have no idea why you have to learn Greek mythology in high school English classes.

Perhaps it's because I hated Greek mythology that I don't remember much of it now. What I do remember is the word *demigod*. A demigod is someone who has the powers of a god but isn't necessarily a god themselves, usually because they're part human.

Some people classify Jesus as a demigod. You can see why, right?

I mean, his mom was human and he's got the powers of a god. So he fits the criteria for a demigod, right?

Maybe.

As we already discussed, despite having God as his father and Mary as his mother, Jesus is fully God and fully human. So he doesn't exactly fit that part of the definition of a demigod.

But what about his power? Does that fit the definition of a demigod?

Jesus definitely had some pretty awesome powers. He changed water into wine. He walked on water. He calmed storms. He multiplied fish and bread. He healed lots of people.

But so did a lot of other people. Just think about some of the Old Testament prophets who also performed miracles. What makes Jesus different from them?

In a nutshell: The source of Jesus' power.

Old Testament prophets performed miracles by tapping into God's power. As a result, their miracles pointed to God's glory, to God's splendor and magnificence. In contrast, Jesus doesn't perform miracles in someone else's name. He commands water to be changed into wine or bread to be multiplied. He uses his touch to rid people of their illnesses. As God, he powers himself and so he gets all the glory—all the honor and praise.

Now, according to the Bible, God's glory is beyond amazing. In one exchange between God and one of the Old Testament heroes of our faith, Moses asks God to show him his glory (Exodus 33:18).

Now before we dig deeper into this story, you need to know that Moses was kind of a big shot. He's the guy who led the Israelites out of Egypt. He parted the Red Sea. He's also the one to whom God gave the Ten Commandments. Yet, in response to Moses' request, God tells him, "You cannot see my face, for no one may see me and live" (Exodus 33:20). In other words, God essentially tells Moses, "I'm God and you're not. I'm perfect, holy, and almighty and you're not. Because of that, there's a huge gap between the two of us."

Despite this, you'd think that if God were going to show his glory to anyone, it'd be Moses—the guy who freed God's chosen people from 400 years of slavery. To say Moses was well-respected by his people—and even the Jews of Jesus' time—is an understatement. Moses was revered.

Even so, Moses wasn't and isn't God. He could point people to God as the source of his power. He could even reflect God's glory to others. But ultimately, since he wasn't God himself, he and God couldn't just sit down and hang out.

Knowing this, God has Moses stand on a rock while he covers him with his hand as his glory passes by. This allows Moses to be in his presence and even to catch a glimpse of his back and yet live to tell about it (Exodus 33:21-22).

Again, that's nice and all. But what about Jesus? Where does his glory come from?

To help us figure this out, let's look at the story of Jesus' transfiguration in Mark 9:2-8.

In this story, Jesus and his closest apostles—Peter, James, and John—go mountain climbing. Once at the top of a high mountain, Jesus' clothes become dazzling white.

Why?

"Thinking of Jesus as a demigod keeps it simple and in terms we understand."

— ANGIE

Because he IS God's glory. As Hebrews 1:3 says, "The Son is the radiance of God's glory and the exact representation of his being, sustaining all things by his powerful word."

As if that's not strange enough, after Jesus becomes dazzling white, dead people start showing up to talk to him. Moses comes, along with another Old Testament prophet, Elijah. Upon seeing them, Peter suggests he and his buddies should build them some shelters.

I don't know about you, but I'm pretty certain had I been on the mountain that day and seen Jesus become dazzling white and dead guys appear, my first words wouldn't have been, "Can I build you a house?"

But that's why context is important. The word *shelters* is actually translated from the Greek word for tabernacle.

So what Peter is really saying here is, "Let's build a tabernacle." That would actually have been a pretty logical Jewish response to this strange event.

Why?

Because that's what the Israelites did after Moses saw God's back— just a small fraction of God's glory. They built a tabernacle—a place to contain and house God's presence so that it could be with them without killing them.

So when Peter says, "Hey, let's build some tabernacles!" he's actually saying "I'm terrified! We've got to find a way to protect ourselves because NO ONE who sees God lives. When this happened before, our ancestors built a tabernacle. Maybe we should do that too."

But they never get the chance. Right after Peter freaks out, a cloud covers everyone and a voice says, "This is my Son, whom I love. Listen to him!" (Mark 9:7).

Now you and I might read that and wonder, "Who said that?"

But Peter, James, and John would have immediately known it was God.

After all, God had shown up in clouds before. In the time of Moses, God led the Israelites through the wilderness as a pillar of clouds (Exodus 13:21).

Knowing this, imagine how terrified Peter, James, and John must have been in this moment, wondering if they'd survive their encounter with God.

Thankfully for them, as quickly as the cloud appears, it disappears. Suddenly, Moses and Elijah disappear as well, leaving only Jesus behind.

> *"Without God's power and glory, Jesus would have been just another prophet."*
> — MATTHEW

Those whose job it was to point others to God are now gone. Their work is finished because God himself has arrived in the person of Jesus.

This Jesus is no mere demigod.

He *is* God—complete with all of God's power and glory.

JESUS Talk

1. How is Jesus similar to a demigod? Different from one?
2. How might it be helpful to your faith to think of Jesus as a demigod? How might it be harmful?
3. What is God's glory?
4. What does it mean to give God all the glory? When/how have you done this?
5. What does it mean that Jesus has all of God's power and glory? Why's it important that he does? Without God's power and glory, how would Jesus' life and ministry have been different?
6. Why does it matter to our faith that Jesus was NOT a demigod, but instead was fully God and fully human?

"Jesus could have died and been crucified on the cross. Had he not also been God, it would not have meant anything."

— ESTHER

10: Both / And

In high school, I participated in Forensics, the speech and debate club. Ever since then, I've been a sucker for good speeches.

Like many Americans, one of my favorite speeches ever is Martin Luther King Jr.'s "I Have a Dream." In it, he casts his vision for the future of America, saying, "I have a dream that one day this nation will rise up and live out the true meaning of its creed: 'We hold these truths to be self-evident: that all men are created equal.' I have a dream that one day on the red hills of Georgia the sons of former slaves and the sons of former slave owners will be able to sit down together at a table of brotherhood."

Any time I hear those words, they give me chills.

His words are just one reason why I think it's impossible NOT to respect the work of Martin Luther King Jr., who was a Southern pastor who became an influential leader during the Civil Rights Movement.

As a pastor, Martin Luther King Jr. followed in the way of Jesus and helped others do the same. Despite the violence he and other African Americans regularly faced, he used nonviolent, peaceful resistance to fight against injustices. He loved others, deeply and radically. His words inspired others to act. He led with grace and dignity. People willingly followed him.

Without a doubt, Martin Luther King Jr. was a good man. He was one of the best leaders the world has ever known.

But that's all he was: a human. No matter how much we respect and, at times, maybe even revere Martin Luther King Jr., he wasn't God.

In contrast, Jesus was.

Jesus was both fully God and fully human.

> "Jesus is the only son of God, one with the Father and the Spirit. He is fully man and fully God."
>
> — SALLY

As a human, Jesus did all the things great leaders like Martin Luther King Jr. did. He used nonviolent, peaceful resistance to fight against the great injustices of his day. He loved others deeply and radically. His words inspired others to act. He led with grace and dignity. People willingly followed him.

But as God, Jesus had power Martin Luther King Jr. lacked. He forgave sins. He taught with authority. He performed miracles. When he was killed, he didn't stay dead. By rising from the grave, he defeated death.

Jesus wasn't human *or* God. He was both.

That's super important. If Jesus was just one or the other—God *or* human—Christianity wouldn't work. It'd be nothing more than a feel-good fad.

If Jesus was just another human, he'd lack the power to forgive our sins.

If Jesus was just another human, he'd have stayed dead... and so would we.

But if Jesus was only God, he'd be unable to relate to and understand us. He'd be completely foreign to us.

Thankfully, in Jesus, we don't have an either/or. We have a both/and.

Like Martin Luther King Jr., Jesus dreamed. He cast a compelling vision for the future.

As God, Jesus will one day make his dreams become reality. He not only casts a compelling vision for the future, he gives us one: a kingdom unlike any the world has ever known.

One in which the last will be first.

> "Jesus was the human form of God. He was fully human, yet fully God. God sent him to die on the cross for our sins, so we may live eternally."
>
> — NICK

One in which there will be no more crying or tears.

One in which all will be made right.

One in which we can and do have a part.

JESUS Talk

1. How is Jesus similar to Martin Luther King Jr.? Other influential leaders?
2. How is Jesus different from Martin Luther King Jr.? Other influential leaders?
3. "If Jesus was just one or the other—God *or* human—Christianity wouldn't work." Why not?
4. When it comes to our faith, why's it important that Jesus was human? God?

Section Three
Was JESUS Really Like Us?

"The second verse of 'Silent Night' really romanticizes Jesus' birth, talking about how he's 'love's pure light' and the 'dawn of redeeming grace.' In reality, he came into the world in the usual way. If he'd descended from heaven or anything else like that, he would've been more of an angel than a savior."

— LIZZIE

11: Not Really a Silent Night

Like many others, my church holds a candlelight service on Christmas Eve. At the end of this service, we light candles and sing "Silent Night." Several hundred people sing

> *Silent night, holy night*
> *All is calm, all is bright*
> *Round yon Virgin Mother and Child*
> *Holy Infant so tender and mild*
> *Sleep in heavenly peace*
> *Sleep in heavenly peace.*

The moment is a beautiful one, though not altogether accurate.

In actuality, Jesus' birth was probably anything but silent. When Jesus was born, there were no hospitals. Instead, people had babies in their homes.

No doubt, that's what Jesus' mother, Mary, expected to do. Until, that is, the Romans—who ruled Jesus' people, the Jews—decided it was time to count everyone in their kingdom. They called for a census and demanded people return to the place where their ancestors were born. For Jesus' parents, this meant traveling from their hometown, Nazareth, to Bethlehem, approximately a three-day trip.

Now, a three-day road trip might not seem like a big deal to you, but as someone who's recently been pregnant, let me tell you, traveling when you're pregnant is ALWAYS a big deal. You're exhausted. Your body aches EVERYWHERE. And you've pretty much got to pee ALL THE TIME. You're miserable. And because you're miserable, so are the people around you.

To make matters worse, this was in the days before Hotwire. So weary and exhausted, Mary and Joseph arrived in Bethlehem with no place to stay.

Luke 2:7 tells us Jesus was born in a stable because there was "no room for them in the inn." This means the night's silence would have been pierced by the cries of all the animals. And by the hustle and bustle of people moving around in an overcrowded city. And by Mary, screaming in pain. And by Jesus' cries after he was born.

Contrary to how we typically imagine this scene, it was also probably not all that lovely.

I mean, Jesus was born in a barn. Even the cleanest barns have traces of animal poop. Not to mention, birth itself is a rather messy affair. There are all kinds of bodily fluids involved—including lots of blood.

"In order to be fully human, Jesus had to be born just like each one of us."

— JANE

Keep in mind that Mary—who we think was probably a teenager like you—had never given birth before. This means she was probably afraid, all the more so because she was away from her home and from the women she loved who would have normally helped her to deliver her baby. Since there were no doctors around, the only person left to help her was Joseph—a carpenter who likely had NO clue how to deliver a baby. Keep in mind that Scripture makes it clear that Joseph "had no union with Mary until she gave birth to a son" (Matthew 1:25, BSB). In other words, helping Mary deliver the baby would likely have been the first time he saw Mary undressed. Talk about awkward.

If you ask me, this sounds like a recipe for chaos, not calm.

Now, it might be tempting to think these details don't matter.

But they do.

When we picture Jesus' birth as "silent" and "calm"- different than a typical human birth -we forget that Jesus came into the world through a very human act. As the apostle Paul says in Philippians 2:7 (NRSVA), Jesus was "born in human likeness; found in human form."

> "Jesus' birth shows us that Jesus came not only to lead us to God but to be one of us."
>
> — SCOTT

This means that Jesus cried—just like you and I did when we were born. He peed—and since he was a boy, he probably accidentally peed all over his parents at least a few times during his infancy. He nursed. He fussed. He cooed. He played. He napped. And he was fully dependent on others for ALL of his needs.

Now to be clear, at his birth, Jesus was also still fully God. This is, I think, what it means when Jesus' friend John tells us in John 1:14, "The Word became flesh and made his dwelling among us."

At Jesus' birth, God became LIKE us.

So even though Jesus' birth wasn't "silent" or all that "calm," God entering the world as a baby boy definitely made it holy.

JESUS Talk:

1. Prior to reading this chapter, how did you picture Jesus' birth? What influenced your picture of Jesus' birth?
2. Why do you think so many Christmas carols, like "Silent Night," ignore the reality of what Jesus' birth would have been like? Why's it important to our faith not to ignore the reality of what Jesus' birth would have been like?
3. To you, what does it mean that Jesus was born fully human, the same way we were? Why's this important to your faith?

"It's hard to be close to Jesus if we view him solely as being a far off image, rather than someone who has experienced pain like we do."

— GREG

12: Dodging bullets

Nestled in the early pages of the Gospel of Matthew is a story we'd rather ignore. It's called the slaughter of the innocents and it's found in Matthew 2:13-16.

It's a story of genocide, of an evil King shamelessly murdering all the babies younger than two years old living in and around Bethlehem.

It seems King Herod launches his ruthless attack in order to eliminate his competition—the baby Jesus, who wise men tell him is "king of the Jews" (Matthew 2:2).

The miracle in this story is that Jesus' family is warned about this impending evil. In a dream, Jesus' earthly dad, Joseph, is told to take his family to Egypt.

So he does.

Perhaps they flee in the middle of the night, like so many of today's refugees do.

As with so many modern day refugees—people forced to flee their country for fear of being persecuted or killed—life in Egypt was hard for Jesus' family. There, Jesus' family would have stood out as foreigners. They would have been unfamiliar with local customs and traditions and separated from their family, friends, and religious community.

The same is true for those who are refugees today. Take, for example, my friend Emile.

Emile is a refugee from the Democratic Republic of Congo, a country in central Africa where war has raged for decades. As a small child Emile and his family were forced to flee to Rwanda, the country that borders the Congo to the east. In doing so, they left behind everything and everyone they knew. They brought with them only a few prized possessions that could be easily carried.

Once in Rwanda, Emile and his family made their way to a refugee camp, where they were given a tarp from the United Nations. This tarp then became the roof of their very small, three-room mud hut. Like all the other homes in the refugee camp, theirs had no electricity, windows, or plumbing.

Because they weren't Rwandan citizens, Emile and his family couldn't work or go to school in Rwanda. Instead, they were forced to depend on meager food rations from the United Nations. Every day for 20 years, they ate the same thing: a little bit of beans and rice.

After nearly 20 years in the refugee camp, Emile and his family were approved for resettlement in the United States by the United Nations. He boarded a plane—which he told me he thought would crash the first time they hit what he now understands to be turbulence. You see, before Emile boarded the plane for his flight to the US, he'd never even seen one, let alone been on one. He had no understanding of how planes worked or what was normal during a flight and what wasn't.

Once in the United States, Emile and his family were resettled in Denver—a place they'd never before heard of. They arrived in the United States in the middle of winter and were stunned by how cold it was, not to mention the snow—something they'd heard of but never seen.

Once in Denver, Emile set out to find a job. He'd always dreamed of becoming an accountant, but his poor English skills limited his options to minimum wage jobs, typically as a custodian.

Despite the difficulty of life in the United States, Emile's faith in Jesus has sustained him. So, too, has his knowledge that, like him, Jesus was a refugee and as a result is able to uniquely understand his suffering.

Now, when I read the horror-filled story of King Herod's massacre of the infants, I often question why it's in Scripture, especially on the heels of the Christmas story. I wonder why God allowed such a horrific event to happen. I mean, it's nice he saved his Son, Jesus, from certain death, but what about all the other babies he didn't save?

In contrast, Emile and other refugees have no doubt why this awful story is in Scripture. It's there to show us that, like us, Jesus knows suffering.

I struggle to understand how suffering can bring people closer to God. I get angry and pull away from a God who lets horrible things happen.

— LINDSEY

Certainly, Jesus suffered on the cross. But as this story shows, Jesus also suffered throughout his life, beginning when he was a baby whose family was forced to flee their homeland lest they be killed. He and his family knew what it meant to be strangers in a strange land. They knew what it meant to be out of place and to stick out like sore thumbs. They knew what it meant to be misunderstood and stereotyped by others who were different from them. They even knew what it meant to fear for their lives.

And maybe that's the real miracle of this story: That through Jesus, God—who is almighty and all-powerful—*knows* suffering, deeply and intimately.

So often suffering confuses us and makes us question God's love.

But that doesn't have to be the case.

Just ask my refugee friends. They're drawn to Jesus precisely *because* he suffered. They're confident that the Kingdom of God isn't just for those who lead a charmed life, but for those, like them, who suffer in profound ways. They know that God's love drew him to suffer alongside us. They're certain that because Jesus suffered, *nothing* can separate them from God. What's more, they trust and believe that through his death and resurrection, one day all suffering will end.

And that's good news that can comfort and sustain us—even when we suffer.

JESUS Talk

1. Have you ever heard someone preach on Herod's massacre of the baby boys? If so, what do you remember about this message? If not, why do you think we don't typically tell this story right alongside the story of the wise men?
2. Jen talked about how she often questions why Herod's massacre is in Scripture. What questions does this story raise for you? Why do you think it's included in Scripture?
3. Who do you know who is currently suffering? How might they find hope in the fact that Jesus also suffered?
4. Describe a time you suffered. How, if at all, did you find comfort in the fact that Jesus suffered?
5. Do you really believe that Jesus' death and resurrection will one day end all suffering? Why or why not?
6. How might you be part of God's Kingdom work to end suffering here and now?

> *"The way we view Jesus and follow in his footsteps changes if we know that he was more like the poor than the rich. This impacts my faith similar to the quote about the camel and the eye of the needle—how it is hard for the wealthy to get into heaven; because it makes me wonder why God has blessed me with so much."*
>
> — JEAN

13: The Homeless Man

My most embarrassing moment as a kid involved my family's car. At the time, we drove an old, rusty beater from the decade before.

One day, my mom drove me to school. As soon as we pulled into the parking lot, the car started making strange noises. The noises got louder and louder, like rapid gunshots. My mom whipped the car into a parking spot and yanked me out, scared that it was actually going to blow up.

Thankfully, it didn't.

But it might as well have. It was just as embarrassing.

You see, the way drop-offs worked at my school is that everyone waited OUTSIDE the school for the building to open. So pretty much the entire school saw my car explode. Needless to say, I was teased relentlessly because of it.

Aside from being embarrassed, this was also the day I realized my family didn't have as much money as other people did. Sure, both my parents worked, but our cars weren't as nice as everyone else's. Our house was smaller than that of my suburban friends. And unlike my friends who seemed to travel to exotic places, our vacations usually consisted of driving across the country to my grandparent's house, 2000 miles away.

the real JESUS

When I entered junior high and high school, I became even more acutely aware of these differences. When I was in seventh grade, my dad was laid off and my mom began working full time. From then on, we had a lot less disposable income than we used to.

Don't get me wrong. My family was far from poor. We lived in a nice house in a safe neighborhood. We had two cars (we just drove them until they exploded). I had plenty of cute clothes. I always attended a private school. My parents even saved enough to pay for my college education. We simply didn't have the money for extras that a lot of my friends' families did. So I saved my babysitting money and eventually got a job. I worked hard and paid for a lot of my weekend activities like going out to the movies or dinner with friends. I also paid for some of my summer trips.

Usually, this didn't bother me. In some ways, it even became a source of pride for me.

But occasionally I felt resentful that none of my other friends had to pay for stuff themselves. To me, it felt like they never had to make any hard choices about what they did. Instead, when they wanted money, they simply asked their parents who provided it.

Somewhere around this time I remember being taught that God provides. Upon hearing this, I remember thinking, "It's awfully easy to believe that God provides when you have everything you want. It's way harder to believe that God provides when money is sometimes an issue for your family."

Later on, the way people linked God's provision with God's blessing made me question why God decided to bless everyone else's families more than mine.

What I wish I knew then was that Jesus' life probably looked far more like mine than that of my wealthy friends.

I mean, Jesus was from a working class family. His dad, Joseph, was a carpenter.

"Knowing Jesus was homeless takes him off his pedestal and also shows how humble he was for not using his godliness to get him earthly things."

— AMANDA

Once Jesus left the family business and began his public ministry, he became completely dependent on the good will and gifts of others in order to survive. For example, Luke 8:3 tells us about a bunch of women who "provided for Jesus out of their resources" (NRSV).

People gave Jesus money, food, and shelter to support his ministry. They did so because as an adult, Jesus was homeless. In Matthew 8:20, he says, "Foxes have holes, and birds of the air have nests; but the Son of Man has nowhere to lay his head."

Even though he was a King, Jesus never lived like royalty. As an adult, he never even had his own house.

Even though he was God, Jesus lived like a human struggling to make ends meet. He could have miraculously made a home for himself out of nothing, but Jesus chose instead to depend on other people's generosity in order to be cared for.

As a result, there were days when Jesus probably wondered where his next meal was coming from. There were nights he no doubt questioned where he would sleep and if he would be safe sleeping there.

But he also trusted God to meet his needs, largely through the kindness and hospitality of others. Doing so joined him together with other people, strengthening his friendships with those whom he depended on. After all, when you live and eat with others, you get to know them differently than if you're just passing acquaintances.

Had my junior high self understood this, I think it would have been much easier for me to stop equating God's blessings with material possessions and instead recognize all the ways in which God met my needs.

"Jesus was God's Son, so he had the power to have anything, live anywhere, and have tons of wealth, but he chose not to. He lived a life similar to the majority of the population, because he truly came for those people."

— CONNOR

My family may not have driven the best cars, but we had everything we needed.

We may not have been wealthy, but our relationships with others definitely made us rich.

JESUS Talk

1. How wealthy is your family? Have you ever had to worry about how your basic needs would be met? If so, what was that experience like for you? Has a lack of finances ever kept you from doing something you wanted to? If so, what was that experience like for you?
2. To you, what does it mean to be blessed? Why do you think we so often equate God's blessings with wealth and material possessions?
3. How does it make you feel to know that Jesus was homeless and that his family was "working class"? How, if at all, do you think this influenced Jesus' teachings? The way he treated the poor?
4. What does Jesus' life teach you about what it means for God to provide?
5. How has God provided for you?
6. If God provides, then how do you explain the times it feels like he doesn't?
7. How might depending on others strengthen your relationship with them?

"It's hard to relate to Jesus because he never sinned. [But] the fact that he faced rejection makes me feel as if he went through the same things as me."

— TAMMY

14: Rejected

The first time I remember being rejected, I was in grade school.

One day, my best friend woke up and decided she no longer liked me. She stopped talking to me and worked hard to make sure no one else did either. At recess, she wouldn't let me hang out with her and her "new" friends. Slowly but surely, she turned all the other girls in our grade against me. Since there were only eight of us, before long, I felt like I had no friends. Most days that year, I left school in tears, unsure of who to trust.

Unfortunately, it's hard to forget those times when we're rejected. Those times—of friend drama or betrayal—stay with us, in many ways scarring us. In the midst of those times, it's easy to feel as though we're the only one who's ever experienced rejection. In reality, everyone's been rejected, including Jesus.

Just before Jesus' crucifixion, nearly all of his closest friends—his apostles—abandon him, afraid that if they stick by his side, they, too, will be put to death.

Before that, Jesus' neighbors and family also reject him. In Luke 4:16-30 we find a bizarre story of Jesus' rejection. One day, Jesus preaches in his hometown synagogue. He quotes a passage from Isaiah about how the "Spirit of the Lord is upon him" and essentially tells everyone, "I'm the one you've been waiting for, the one who

God has sent to fulfill the Scriptures." This upsets all who hear it, so much so that his neighbors attempt to hurl Jesus off a cliff.

Clearly, they don't succeed. Jesus is, however, run out of town.

Elsewhere in Scripture, in Mark 3:21, we're told how early in Jesus' ministry, his family tries to "restrain him" because those in his hometown think he's crazy, possessed by the "ruler of the demons he casts out" (ISV).

Now, it's possible that Jesus' family has good reasons for trying to restrain him. They might be trying to protect him. After all, if the town thinks he's crazy, who's to say people won't try to harm Jesus? Beyond that, Jesus' family might worry about their own well-being.

"People rejected Jesus because they didn't understand him."

— NATHANIEL

If the townspeople think Jesus is crazy, they'll probably stop using the family business for all their carpentry needs. Without the family business, how will they survive?

Regardless of the reasons, Scripture is clear. Jesus' own family rejects him. So he knows what it feels like to be rejected, not just at the end of his life but throughout it.

He knows how painful it is to have the people you most love suddenly turn against you. He understands what it's like to feel like everyone fits in except for you. He knows what it's like to be called hurtful names like "crazy."

Since Jesus has experienced rejection himself, whenever we face rejection, we can go to him, unashamedly telling him how much it hurts, confident that because he's been there, he understands.

That may not feel like much until you realize this: Since Jesus was human, he knows our pain. He can empathize with us. He cares deeply about all aspects of our lives—the big and small stuff.

"If you can't relate to Jesus, you can't know, love, and learn from him."

— ELAINE

That's pretty remarkable when you realize Jesus is also fully God. Since he is, that means we don't worship a distant god, but one who is—in every way—approachable.

So next time you face rejection, don't hesitate to tell Jesus.

After all, he's been there too.

JESUS Talk

1. Describe a time when you experienced rejection.
2. Often, it feels like God is absent from the hard times in our life, like when we're rejected. Think about your life. When have you experienced the feeling of God's absence?
3. Jen encouraged you to talk to Jesus about those times you've been rejected. What might prohibit you from doing so? What might you gain from doing so?
4. In Jesus, we worship an approachable God. How would Christianity be different if we worshiped a distant God?
5. How does knowing Jesus also faced rejection help you relate to him? Why's it important for you to be able to relate to Jesus?

*"Jesus is saving us from being broken or sad.
We can still feel sad.
He's still always there."*

— DIANA

15: Cry Baby

We buried my Grandma on the day that, 81 years before, she'd been born. She had died on my kitchen floor four days earlier. In the days immediately following her death, what I remember is this: Most things people said weren't helpful. People told me…

> *"Your grandma is in a better place."*
> *"At least now, your grandma's not suffering."*
> *"God must have wanted another angel."*

No matter how comforting these things were meant to be, I can assure you they weren't. To my 14-year-old self, the promise of heaven wasn't very reassuring. I didn't care that my grandma was with Jesus; I wanted her to be with me.

The most helpful thing someone said to me during those early days was actually NOTHING.

That's right. Nothing.

Rather than talk, my youth pastor came and hugged me. Then she sat with me as I cried. In that moment, she offered me the gift of her presence. It was incredibly powerful.

Little did I know, she learned to do that from Jesus.

In John 11, we learn of the death of Jesus' close friend Lazarus. After Lazarus's death, Jesus goes to his friend's home, where he finds Lazarus' sisters, Mary and Martha, inconsolable—in tears, grieving the loss of their beloved brother. When Jesus sees their tears, he asks one question: "Where have you laid him?"

"Jesus is someone who will always be there, whether you know it or not."

— GRACE

He does not, however, offer them any empty words.

Instead, he does what any person would do in the wake of their friend's death.

He weeps.

He does so even though he is also God, and as God, Jesus knows how this story will end. He knows that in just a few short minutes, he'll raise Lazarus from the dead.

Even so, he doesn't try to comfort Mary and Martha with words. He simply joins them in their sorrow, weeping with them and offering them the gift of his presence.

In the same way, Jesus weeps with us.

When those close to us die, Jesus weeps.

When natural disasters strike, Jesus weeps.

"Jesus saved us from sadness. We're comforted by [Jesus] when a family member dies or you don't get the job."

— MIKE

When our parents lose their jobs and we're scared what will happen to our family, Jesus weeps.

In other words, whenever we face tragedy or sorrow of any sort, Jesus weeps with and for us. And he does so even though he knows that death and sorrow are never the ending of our stories.

After all, through his own death and resurrection, Jesus conquered death and is, even now, making all things new.

JESUS Talk

1. Describe your first encounter with death.
2. To you, what does it mean that Jesus weeps with us?
3. How does it make you feel to know that Jesus weeps with you?
4. Why's it important that Jesus weeps with us—even though he knows the ending of our stories?
5. To you, what does it mean that Jesus is making all things new?
6. What evidence do you see in the world around you that Jesus is making all things new?

> *"Sometimes we only talk to Jesus when we sin or do something wrong or want something, instead of turning to him in all our times of trial."*
>
> — REBECCA

16: Call Me

I have a confession to make.

Prayer is hard for me.

It's not a part of faith that comes naturally to me. In fact, prayer typically feels pretty strange to me. It often feels more like I'm talking to myself than anything else. Yet, I do it because Jesus did it and we're supposed to follow his example.

Since we're being honest with each other, though, let me just say: When it comes to prayer, I think Jesus' example is far more confusing than helpful.

I mean, think about this. One of the ways I learned to pray was by using the acronym ACTS:

Adoration
Confession
Thanksgiving
Supplication

According to this model, we begin prayer by telling God how awesome he is. Then we confess our sins. Next we give thanks to God for all the ways he's at work in our lives. Finally, we ask God for what we need (that's what it means to supplicate).

I can see where it makes sense for me to pray like this. But how does it make sense for Jesus?

Since Jesus *is* God, wouldn't it be a little strange for him to begin prayer by telling himself how awesome he is? I mean, does he really need to boost his own ego like that?

Since Jesus *is* God, he also has no need for confession. After all, he's perfect. He never sinned so he has no wrongdoings to admit to or ask forgiveness for.

Since Jesus *is* God, why does he need to give thanks to God? Isn't that just giving thanks to himself?

And since Jesus *is* God, why does he need to ask himself for what he needs? Doesn't he already know that?

And that, in a nutshell, is what's so confusing to me about Jesus and prayer. When Jesus prays, is he just talking to himself? Is he like a crazy man playing the role of both God the Son and God the Father?

To answer these questions, let's look at some of the times in Scripture when Jesus prays.

Throughout the four Gospels—the New Testament books written about Jesus—Jesus often prays for others, including the little children whom he blesses (Matthew 19:13). In the longest recorded prayer we have of Jesus', found in John 17, Jesus prays specifically for his apostles before then praying for all believers.

Jesus also prays a lot before or after stressful situations. Before choosing his 12 apostles, Jesus spends an entire night in prayer (Luke 6:12). After the brutal beheading of his cousin John, he miraculously feeds 5000 people and then escapes, alone, to pray (Matthew 14:23). Immediately before his arrest and crucifixion, he goes off to pray in the garden of Gethsemane. There, he begs the Father NOT to make him die but also commits himself to doing the Father's will, saying, "My Father, if it is possible, may this cup be taken from me. Yet not as I will, but as you will" (Matthew 26:39). According to Luke, this prayer is so emotional for Jesus that "his sweat was like drops of blood falling to the ground" (Luke 22:44).

What strikes me about each of these instances is that for Jesus, prayer seems to be far more about communicating with his Dad than anything else. For Jesus, prayer seems a lot like calling a trusted family member or friend to talk about whatever's on his mind.

For example, I frequently call or text my husband while he's at work. Sometimes something happens that's exciting that I can't wait to tell him about. Other times, I'm frustrated and need to vent. Still other times, I want to talk through a problem with him—not because I can't figure out a solution on my own but because I value our relationship, and so I want to talk through important things with him.

It's the same with Jesus who, because he values his relationship with his Father, wants to talk to him—about whatever's currently going on in his life. For Jesus, prayer is about deepening his relationship with his Dad. It's not about getting his way or even about getting some specific result. I mean, as God, he already knows the future and as his prayer in Gethsemane shows, he's committed to it—no matter how hard it might be for him.

So like us, Jesus prays.

But unlike us, he doesn't do so in order to get God the Father to forgive his sins (because he has none) or grant his requests.

Instead when Jesus prays—since he, too, *is* God—he prays to God the Father from a position of equality. For him, prayer is simply a way of checking in and talking to his Dad.

What's amazing is that because of Jesus, even though we're far from God's equal, prayer is still the same thing for us: a way of checking in and talking to our Heavenly Father—not just because we need his forgiveness or help, but because we want to spill our guts to the one who knows and cares for us more than anyone else.

JESUS Talk

1. For you, how easy or difficult is prayer? Why do you think this is?
2. Think about prayer in terms of the ACTS model. Which part of prayer (Adoration, Confession, Thanksgiving, or Supplication) is easiest for you? Hardest? Why do you think this is?
3. How do you think Jesus' prayers strengthened his relationship with God the Father? How might your prayers enable you to do the same?
4. If prayer is really about deepening our relationship with God, then what should you pray about?

Section Four
What Did JESUS Do?

"There's a verse—he taught as one who had authority. Jesus spits out all this crazy wisdom and beauty. He talked to people."
— AMY

17: JESUS Taught

I was always a good kid... until, that is, I started questioning people's authority.

My sophomore year in high school, my church got a new youth pastor. To say I wasn't his greatest fan is an understatement. I spent the year questioning him and his authority. Among other things, I wondered why I had to listen to this guy. Often I was given the very unsatisfactory answer, "Because he's your pastor."

My senior year in high school, I was co-editor of our school's newspaper. As part of our job, my co-editor and I often wrote the paper's unsigned editorial. We spent the year questioning people's authority: our harebrained guidance counselor, one of the deans for instituting a "mandatory" fundraiser, and the chair of the English department, who started censoring the paper in response to our earlier editorials. That year, I had frequent run-ins with our school's principal who didn't like having her authority—or the authority of her staff—questioned.

Given my track record, maybe it comes as no surprise to you that during high school, I spent a lot of time questioning my faith and in particular, the words and teachings of Jesus. I wasn't content believing in Jesus just because someone else told me to. I wanted to know why his words could be trusted. I wanted to know what, if any, authority Jesus really had.

Today, people's authority tends to come from their education, position, and the amount of followers they have. According to these measures, Jesus had virtually no authority.

Before he started his public ministry, Jesus worked in the family business. This means he probably wasn't a great student. Had he been, a local rabbi would have invited Jesus to study with him.

Jesus also had no real position. His parents weren't married when he was born. His dad was a tradesman. To make matters worse, Jesus was from Nazareth, which had a poor reputation. As a man by the name of Nathaniel once said, "Nazareth! Can anything good come from there?" (John 1:46).

What's more, according to Scripture, Jesus only had 12 apostles. Even I have more Twitter followers than that.

Yet, Mark 1:21-22 tells us how when Jesus taught he did so "as one having authority"—something that astounded those who heard him.

Clearly, Jesus' authority didn't come from the usual things: a great education, prestigious position, or huge number of followers. It came from something—or someone—else.

God.

In John 10:30, Jesus tells his disciples, "I and the Father are one."

That's right. They're one. If the Father is God, then Jesus is too.

Jesus teaches with authority because as God, he *is* the ultimate authority. Using only his words, he created the world.

Now, maybe to you that feels a little bit like asking, "Why do we have to listen to this guy?" only to be told, "Because he's in charge."

That's incredibly unsatisfying.

Trust me. I know; I've been there.

Fortunately, in Jesus' case, we've got something more than empty words to authenticate his authority. You see, Jesus' life—and the changed lives of others—are evidence of his authority.

Jesus lived what he preached—even when it came to the hard things. He taught his followers to "Love your enemies and pray for those who persecute you" (Matthew 5:44). Then he actually did it. While dying on the cross, Jesus pleaded with God the Father to forgive those who were crucifying him (Luke 23:34).

The changed lives of others also attest to Jesus' authority. Take, for example, the story of Zacchaeus, a wealthy tax collector. Like other tax collectors, Zacchaeus made his money robbing people. He'd charge people the amount of the tax plus some extra, which he'd pocket for himself. Despite this, when Jesus comes to town, Zacchaeus wants desperately to catch a glimpse of him. So he climbs up into a tree. Jesus spots him there and invites himself over for dinner. Zacchaeus welcomes him into his house and is changed. He gives half his stuff to the poor and pays back those he's cheated— four times as much he stole from them (Luke 19:1-10).

Jesus' teachings change Zacchaeus and lots of other people like him. Those transformed lives speak to Jesus' authority.

Still not satisfied?

Then go ahead.

Read the red stuff—Jesus' words—in Scripture. As you do, ask yourself, "How can someone who isn't God not only say these words, but live them out as well? How can the words of someone who isn't God transform the lives of others as much as Jesus' did?"

As you wrestle with these things, take heart. Questioning Jesus' authority won't make you a bad person or even a bad Christian.

It might actually make you a better one.

After all, when you study Jesus' teachings, you just might be changed by them yourself.

JESUS Talk

1. When it comes to your faith, what have you or do you question? Why?
2. When it comes to Jesus' words, what have you or do you question? Why?
3. Do you believe God is the ultimate authority? Why or why not?
4. How are Jesus' life and the changed lives of others evidence of his authority?
5. How might questioning Jesus' authority make you a better Christian?
6. How have you been changed by Jesus' words?
7. How do Jesus' teachings show he is God?

> "Jesus forgiving our sins is the ultimate thing. He opened up the path to heaven, even if we don't live a perfect life."
>
> — RYAN

18: **JESUS** Forgave.

My senior class chose the Beatles song "With a Little Help from My Friends" as our class song. We chose it in order to represent the way our class had connected and supported one another throughout our four years of high school.

In spite of that, whenever I hear this song, that's not typically what I think about.

Instead, I think about a story embedded in the first few pages of the Gospel of Mark. It's a story in which four guys carry their paralyzed friend to Jesus, hoping against hope that Jesus will heal their friend and enable him to walk.

The problem is that when these men arrive on the scene, the house where Jesus is hanging out is packed—so crowded that they can't get anywhere near Jesus. Out of desperation, they do whatever it is they need to do in order to get their friend to Jesus.

They cut a hole in the roof and lower their paralyzed friend down.

When Jesus sees the paralyzed man, he immediately tells him, "Your sins are forgiven."

Truth be told, this has always struck me as odd.

What this man—and his friends—want most is for him to be healed, for him to be able to walk again. Instead, Jesus forgives him and in the process, greatly upsets the religious leaders.

The religious leaders accuse Jesus of blasphemy, or showing contempt for God. In their words, "Who can forgive sins but God alone?" (Mark 2:1-12).

You see, the only person who has the authority to forgive a sin is the one who's been wronged.

Here's what I mean. When I was in college, my parents came for a visit. While there, my mom and my fiancé, Doug, got into a huge fight.

Initially, I was oblivious to the problem. But then, my mom's mood began to rapidly deteriorate. Eventually Doug left, and I asked her what was wrong. She said Doug had done something that had greatly offended and upset her. Not wanting two of the most important people in my life to be angry with one another, I called Doug in tears.

He apologized to me, which I very much appreciated.

The problem is—I wasn't the one he'd screwed things up with. I wasn't the one who Doug had sinned against. That was my mom.

Doug knew this, and so he called my mom, apologized, and did a fair amount of groveling. My mom graciously forgave him, something only she could do.

In the same way, only God has the authority to truly forgive our sins, because ultimately all our sins are against him. So when Jesus tells this paralyzed man, "Your sins are forgiven," he's essentially saying, "I can forgive your sins because all of your sins are against me." In other words, Jesus is saying he's God and that as God, he's got the authority to forgive our sins.

It's a bold claim that he makes whenever he offers people—including us—forgiveness.

Now, since I don't want to leave you hanging, let me assure you Jesus also gives the paralyzed man what he originally wanted: He heals him. The formerly paralyzed man then gets up and walks out in front of all his family and friends.

His ability to walk proves he's been healed physically. It's outward proof of the inward healing he's experienced because Jesus—the God of the Universe—has forgiven his sins.

Thanks to Jesus, this man's healing is deep.

So is ours when we, too, experience his forgiveness.

JESUS Talk

1. What does it mean that the only person who has the authority to forgive sins is the person who's been wronged?
2. Ultimately, how are all our sins against God?
3. The paralyzed man's ability to walk shows proof that he's been forgiven. What proof do we have that we've been forgiven?
4. How does God's forgiveness heal us?
5. How does Jesus' ability to forgive show he's God?

> *"We already knew that God can cause huge storms and floods, so it's comforting to know he also can calm them."*
>
> — MAX

19: **JESUS** Performed Miracles

When I was in high school, my church took yearly canoe trips to the Boundary Waters. In case you've never gotten the chance to explore the Boundary Waters in northern Minnesota, let me describe them for you.

It's untouched wilderness filled with bears, moose, and other wildlife. The only way to explore it is by canoe.

Campsites are rustic: a clearing in the woods marked by a fire pit and a latrine. Not an outhouse—just a latrine. A plastic toilet out in the open, in the middle of the woods. What you pack in, you pack out. There are no garbage cans along the way.

You're miles from civilization and, in some cases, people. It's possible to go days without seeing anyone else. It's also extraordinary beautiful.

During our canoe trips, we'd paddle several miles a day, explore the beauty of the Boundary Waters, and camp. It was great fun, so much so that it was always one of my favorite weeks of the year.

During one of our canoe trips, we encountered a horrible storm. The wind was so strong that it whipped up waves two feet high.

Now, for those of you who have taken cruises, such waves are probably no big deal. But to a canoeist, waves that high are a *very* big deal. In addition to constantly throwing you off course and making it insanely difficult to paddle, such waves are dangerous. They can easily swamp your canoe and cause it to tip. In a storm that size, one thing you definitely don't want to do is go for an unexpected swim.

Knowing this, as soon as the storm started our trip leader, Scott, decided to get us to shore. We dug our paddles into the water hard, canoeing diagonally across the waves in order to minimize our chances of tipping. We inched forward, only to have the wind push us backwards. It was agonizingly slow progress, but eventually we made it to shore, sopping wet and cold.

In order to warm us up once ashore, Scott decided we should eat lunch. The only problem was that required water. Back in the day, we didn't filter the water. We simply got it from the middle of the lake, believing it to be cleaner than shore water.

Not wanting to send any of us into harm's way, Scott chose to fetch the water himself. In normal water, when a lone person gets in a canoe, they get in the rear seat and paddle from there. That day, that's not what Scott—an experienced canoeist—did. Instead, he put on a life vest (something he never wore), got into the middle of the canoe, and knelt—all in an effort to reduce the likelihood he'd tip.

Seeing Scott take those extra precautions made me realize he was afraid. That, in turn, made me fearful. I worried something would happen to Scott on his water run and that we'd be left alone—without the ability to find our way back to civilization. I worried about the bears I knew lurked in the woods. Earlier that week, one had run into our campsite, and it was terrifying. I worried what would happen if the storm continued. Sure, we were on the shore, but we weren't at a campsite. There wasn't room for us to pitch a tent, nor was their adequate shelter of any kind. I knew that without shelter, hypothermia was a very real danger.

the real**JESUS**

With every second Scott was gone, I was more and more convinced we were all going to die. I was, in a word, terrified.

Because of how much that storm terrified me, I can relate—at least a little—to the fear Jesus' apostles feel when they, too, get caught in a storm on the Sea of Galilee. Mark 4:37 describes this storm as a "furious squall" with waves so high that it leaves the disciples' boat "nearly swamped." We might describe this storm as one that's hurricane-like. It's so bad that when Jesus' disciples find him asleep, they frantically wake him up, shouting, "Don't you care if we drown?"

That the apostles—many of whom were professional fishermen who'd grown up on the water—think they can actually drown in this storm shows just how bad it is.

They're terrified.

> "If Jesus can calm a hurricane, he can protect me from some stressful tests!"
>
> — JENNIFER

Fortunately for them, Jesus doesn't share their fear. He calmly gets up and tells this hurricane-like storm, "Quiet! Be still!"

Like a child obeying her parents, the storm obeys Jesus. The waves die down, and immediately the entire sea becomes "completely calm."

Now, if you've ever been caught in a storm, you know that's not typically how this works. Most storms die down gradually; it takes hours for the water to become completely calm after a storm.

That's certainly what happened that day on our canoe trip. Once Scott decided it was safe enough for us to continue on to that night's camping destination, we still encountered waves. They weren't large enough to make canoeing dangerous anymore, but they were big enough to make it hard.

As experienced fishermen, Jesus' disciples knew that too. Sea as smooth as glass immediately after a hurricane-like storm would definitely have gotten their attention. That's when Jesus asks them, "Why are you so afraid?"

Often, I think we read this question and assume Jesus is upset with his disciples, who never quite seem to understand what's happening. But I wonder if something else is going on here. I wonder if, instead, Jesus is reminding them (and us!) that with him in the boat, there's no reason to be afraid. After all, what's important is not the strength of the storm or the strength of the boat or even our own strength. What's important is Jesus' strength. Clearly he has the power to calm storms.

That's significant—especially to people who believed that the only one who could control the sea was God. By calming the storm using only his words, Jesus is, therefore, claiming to be God. According to Pastor Timothy Keller, it's like Jesus is saying, "I am not just someone who has power; I am power itself. Anyone and anything in the whole universe that has any power has it on loan from me."[1]

"No matter how crazy my life can get, Jesus can always calm it."

— MADDIE

It's Jesus' power to calm the storm using only his words that make his friends question, "Who is this? Even the wind and the waves obey him!" (Mark 4:35-41).

No wonder Mark 4:41 says that even *after* Jesus calms the storm, the apostles are "terrified." Before they were terrified because they thought they were going to drown in a storm they couldn't control.

---

1. Timothy Keller, *Jesus the King* (Riverhead, 2011), 55.

But after the storm, they're even more terrified because they've learned they can't control Jesus—who has far more power than even a hurricane-like storm.

Maybe that should be our reaction to Jesus as well.

I mean, it's reassuring that Jesus can calm the storm, but let's be honest. It's also terrifying.

If Jesus can calm the storm, then he's God. And if Jesus is God, as much as he's like us, he cannot be controlled.

We can't make him into our own image. We can't put him into a box. We can't think we have him figured out.

As this miracle demonstrates, as much as we might try, we cannot control Jesus, who is God. In actuality, he's the one who's always in control.

JESUS Talk

1. Describe a time when, like Jen, you've been caught in a storm. How did that experience make you feel?
2. Be honest. To you, is it more reassuring or terrifying that Jesus can calm storms? Why?
3. What's a "storm" you're currently going through in your life? Do you really believe that Jesus has the power to calm it? Why or why not?
4. In what ways do you try to control Jesus? What evidence have you seen that he's actually in control of your life?
5. How do Jesus' miracles show he is God?

"I love the idea that it's up to us to continue the story of Jesus! The story of the resurrection isn't just a story that happened 2000 years ago, it's a story that's kept alive through us. We bring life to the world every time we give our time or money to serve others, every time we see and love others as Jesus does, and every time we share the story of Jesus and invite someone to follow him."

— STEPHANIE

20: JESUS Rose from the Dead

I love musical theater. As a child, one of the things my family consistently splurged on was going to see musicals in downtown Chicago. When we weren't watching live theater, we were listening to recordings of it at home.

Part of my family's Easter tradition was watching Andrew Lloyd Webber's *Jesus Christ Superstar* each year on Good Friday. To this day, I can quote parts of the Holy Week story—not because I've been diligent about memorizing Scripture, but because they're lines found in *Jesus Christ Superstar*.

My senior year in college, I was beyond thrilled to co-direct a production of *Jesus Christ Superstar* with a good friend. We did so through a student organization called the Christian Theater Music Club.

As word spread to the surrounding community about what we were doing, several churches approached us, concerned over the fact that a Christian organization was doing a production of *Jesus Christ Superstar*. You see, while *Jesus Christ Superstar* showcases the events of Holy Week including Jesus' triumphal entry into Jerusalem, the Last Supper, and Jesus' arrest, trial, and execution, it's told from the perspective of Judas—the apostle who betrayed him. It also ends, not with Jesus' resurrection, but with his death. (That's the reason my family always watched it on Good Friday and not on Easter.) For that reason, many Christians find *Jesus Christ Superstar* offensive, or at least incomplete.

In response to this criticism, we assured people that we had every intention of completing the story by depicting the Resurrection during the show's final song.

That said, at the start of tech week—the week before the show opened—we still had not figured out how we were going to do it. Mark—a good friend of mine and the guy playing Jesus—approached me that Monday, visibly upset, saying, "When are we going to figure this out, Jen? Without the Resurrection, everything else is pointless."

Indeed, it is.

Had Jesus not risen from the dead, he would have been just like other religious leaders—good teachers who eventually died and stayed dead.

But that's not what happens.

After his death, Jesus is laid to rest in a cave. After the Sabbath is over, some of his followers return to Jesus' tomb in order to anoint his body, an important Jewish custom. When the women arrive at the tomb, they find the stone rolled away and the tomb empty except for a "young man dressed in a white robe" sitting where Jesus' body should have been.

The women are understandably alarmed but the man explains, "You are looking for Jesus the Nazarene who was crucified. He has risen! He is not here" (Mark 16:1-6).

On that Easter morning some 2000 years ago, everything changed. Jesus conquered death—the last thing separating us from God the Father. In doing so, he showed us what he meant when, after the death of her brother Lazarus, Jesus tells Martha, "I am the resurrection and the life. He who believes in me will live, even though he dies, and whoever lives and believes in me will never die" (John 11:25-26, BSB).

The first two words in this sentence are especially significant: *I am.*

This is the name that God the Father gave himself centuries before, in a conversation with Moses (Exodus 3:14).

I am who I am.

So when Jesus says, "I am the resurrection and the life," he's saying two things:

1. "Make no mistake, I'm God."
2. "Because I'm God, I can bring dead things back to life. Through me, death has been defeated."

In Jesus' resurrection, we see proof that his words are true.

Jesus' resurrection becomes a preview for what he's promised his followers: One day, we too, will rise and have eternal life.

My friend Mark was right all those years ago when, in the process of working on *Jesus Christ Superstar,* he told me that without the resurrection, the rest of the story is pointless. The foundation of the Christian faith is indeed Jesus' resurrection. For that reason, we found a way to include it in our version of *Jesus Christ Superstar* (along with a dry ice machine and some fancy up-lighting.)

But here's the thing. Even though we did, our story was still incomplete.

Even though the resurrection is near the end of Jesus' story, it's at the beginning of ours. Just look at the Gospel of Mark, which essentially has two endings. The first ends with the women fleeing the tomb, terrified by what they'd just seen and heard. The second features Jesus appearing to his disciples and telling them to go make disciples before he then ascends to heaven.

Most scholars believe the second ending, the one that's much more of a "happily ever after," was added much later and that the first ending—the one with the terrified women—is probably Mark's original ending.

The original ending is largely unsatisfying. It's incomplete and unresolved. We're left with far more questions than answers, feeling like, "Wait! The story can't end here. What happens next?"

And maybe that's the point.

Although Jesus' resurrection is the foundation of Christianity, it's not the end of the story.

We are.

In Jesus, we see that God is in the business of bringing dead things back to life. As followers of Jesus, we're in that same business. We're called to continue Jesus' work in the world. So how are you bringing life to the world around you?

Whenever you bring life to the world around you, you're helping to complete the story.

Without Jesus' resurrection, Christianity is pointless. But without you to continue Jesus' work in the world, the Christian story is unfinished.

JESUS Talk

1. Do you agree or disagree that without the resurrection, everything else in Jesus' story is pointless? Why?
2. According to Jen, "Even though the resurrection is near the end of Jesus' story, it's at the beginning of ours." As followers of Jesus, why's this important for us to remember?
3. Answer Jen's question, "How are you bringing life to the world around you?"
4. How does Jesus' resurrection show that he is God?

Section Five
Did JESUS Teach...?

> "Jesus set the basis for what we now follow as Christians. Our holidays and major moments are based off of moments in his life, things he couldn't have taught because they hadn't happened."
> — CLAIRE

21: Did JESUS Teach Christianity?

I've always been a good student; I've never been a good test taker. Maybe you can relate.

One reason for this is that I tend to overanalyze things. I see potential pitfalls absolutely everywhere, even in simple types of questions, like true or false. Take for example, this one:

True or False? Jesus taught Christianity.

If this question were on a test, I'd spend far too long analyzing it, considering every possible angle in my attempt to get it "right."

On the one hand, Jesus definitely taught Christianity. I mean, we look to him as our ultimate example of how to live. As his followers, we try to do what he did and live out what he taught.

On the other hand, Jesus couldn't have taught Christianity. I mean, he was Jewish, not Christian. He was raised by Jewish parents who descended from the equivalent of Jewish royalty—King David himself (Matthew 1:1-16). Jesus' parents, Mary and Joseph, followed Jewish customs while raising Jesus. For example, when he was eight days old, Jesus' parents, Mary and Joseph, circumcised him and formally named him (Luke 2:21), in keeping with Jewish tradition. Since he was Jewish, Jesus also didn't grow up celebrating Christian holidays like we do. Instead of celebrating Christmas, he and his family would have celebrated Hanukkah, a festival that lasts eight days and commemorates the rededication of the Temple in 165 BC after its desecration by the Syrians.

Similarly, instead of celebrating Easter, Jesus' family would have celebrated Passover, like thousands of Jews did before them. During this festival, they would have remembered the 10 plagues and in particular how the Lord passed over the homes of the Israelites and spared their firstborn sons from the angel of death. They would have celebrated the Israelites' freedom from slavery in Egypt (Exodus 12:1-28).

Not only would these holidays have been yearly traditions in Jesus' home growing up, but Jesus would have continued celebrating these traditional Jewish festivals as an adult. In fact, that's what he and his followers were doing when they gathered for their last meal together right before Jesus' death (Matthew 26:17-25).

> "Jesus' heritage reminds you that he didn't set out to create Christianity, it just happened that way."
>
> — ELIJAH

Jesus was Jewish, through and through.

Jesus' intent was never to begin a new religion. Jesus didn't come to "abolish the law or the prophets" but to fulfill them (Matthew 5:17). He modeled what it actually meant to keep and practice the Jewish laws perfectly, but he did so in a way that often defied the religious leaders' expectations and interpretations of them. For example, for centuries Jews had been taught "eye for eye and tooth for tooth" (Matthew 5:38). Originally, this law was created to prevent overreactions to crimes. For example, killing someone for stealing a loaf of bread. Jesus interpreted this very differently though. According to him, we're supposed to repay violence with kindness by doing things like turning the other cheek. This created a lot of conflict between Jesus and the prominent religious leaders of the day, who were often far more concerned with following the letter of the law than the spirit of it. Jesus also commonly butted heads with religious leaders who didn't much care for the fact that Jesus seemed more concerned with letting people into their religious circles than keeping them out. In Jesus' own words, he came "to call not the righteous but sinners," since "those who are well have no need of a physician" (Mark 2:17, ESV). Jesus cared far more about loving people than about starting a new, Christian religion. It's his followers who did that after his death and resurrection.

"He was trying to start a way of life and then people caught on to it."

— EMMA

In the same way, while Jesus' words are found in the New Testament and, in particular, in the four Gospels (Matthew, Mark, Luke, John) that tell his story, Jesus couldn't have actually taught from the New Testament. It didn't exist in his day. Instead, when he quoted Scripture, he would have been referencing sacred Jewish texts— many of which are found in our Old Testament.

Given all of this, I'd have to conclude that the statement *Jesus taught Christianity* is false.

While Christianity is based on Jesus' teachings, Christianity as a religion didn't form until years after Jesus' resurrection.

There's no way then that Jesus could have taught it. How could he have when it didn't yet exist?

JESUS Talk

1. How would the world that Jesus lived in have been different than our own?
2. How is Jesus' Jewish heritage reflected in his life and teachings?
3. Although Jesus didn't teach Christianity, his words and life are the basis of Christianity. How?
4. Jen argues that Jesus' intent wasn't to start a new religion. Do you agree or disagree? Why?
5. If Jesus didn't teach Christianity, who did? How did Christianity come to be?
6. How do you think Jesus feels about Christianity, the religion that now bears his name? Why?

"Jesus taught us to follow God and worry not about how to earn your faith, but to trust that God is always there."

— JACK

22: Did **JESUS** Teach that Good Works Will Save You?

My maiden name is Nelson. When I was in high school, there was a senior with the same name: Jen Nelson. I knew nothing about this girl except that she was frequently in trouble. At least once a month, I'd hear this over the school's loud speaker:

Paging Jen Nelson to the principal's office.

Every time I heard this, I'd freak out.

You see, I'm a perpetual rule follower. I have a VERY hard time breaking rules for any reason. I find comfort in the structure that rules provide. For this reason, it stressed me out to think that I might have inadvertently broken a rule at school.

Because I'm such a rule follower, I can relate at least a little to the rich young man in Matthew 19:16 who asks Jesus, "What good thing must I do to get eternal life?"

In response to this man, Jesus says, "If you want to enter life, obey the commandments" (Matthew 19:17). In other words, follow the rules.

Like me, this rich young man is a perpetual rule follower. Naturally, he wants to be sure he's doing what he's supposed to do. So he asks Jesus, "Which ones?" (Matthew 19:18).

In response, Jesus recites some of the Ten Commandments:

Do not murder.
Do not commit adultery.
Do not steal.
Do not give false testimony.
Honor your father and mother.
And love your neighbor as yourself.

As Jesus is reciting these commandments (Matthew 19:18), the rich young man is no doubt standing there keeping a mental checklist. (As a fellow rule follower, that's what I would have done). Having successfully checked off ALL the things Jesus mentions, as soon as Jesus finishes speaking, the rich young man lets out a deep sigh of relief and says quite honestly (but not so humbly), "Nailed it! I've done ALL of those things."

But like all rule followers, this guy wants to make sure nothing's slipped through the cracks. Just to be sure he's good to go, he asks Jesus his question in another way, "What do I still lack?" (Matthew 19:20).

"Jesus taught us to do good works to be closer to God."

— CAROLINE

Now before we get to Jesus' answer to this question, take a look at the list of commandments Jesus initially recites to the rich young man. You'll notice it's missing four of the Ten Commandments, including an entire section: the one that pertains to our relationship with God.

In his initial conversation with the rich young man, Jesus never mentions the importance of putting God first, avoiding idols, or not taking God's name in vain. But he's about to.

Jesus tells the rule follower, "If you want to be perfect, go, sell your possessions and give to the poor and you will have treasure in heaven. Then come, follow me" (Matthew 19:21).

To put it another way, Jesus tells this guy, "Don't think I forgot about those other commandments. Remember how you're not supposed to have idols or put things ahead of God? Well, you've made your wealth and possessions an idol. So if you truly want to follow me, get rid of those things."

This must have crushed the rich young man, who was convinced he'd successfully followed all of the rules. No wonder he goes away sad (Matthew 19:22).

As a fellow rule follower, this story certainly crushes me, especially since it feels like Jesus is saying good works will save you. In reality, though, that's not what Jesus is saying at all.

You see, Matthew—the author of this Gospel—was writing to the Jewish people, who didn't view heaven the way we do: as a place of eternal paradise you go to after you die. Instead, they thought of heaven as a time in the future when God would make everything right with the world, when he'd fix all injustices. In the same way, Matthew's readers would not have interpreted *perfect* in the same way we do: as the absence of sin. Instead, they would have thought of being perfect as being complete.

With that in mind, when Matthew's initial readers heard Jesus' words to the rich young man, they'd have interpreted them much differently than we do. To them, Jesus' words would have meant something like, "If you want to be complete, go, sell your possessions and give to the poor. Then you'll be part of my Kingdom, right here, right now."

Now, maybe to you that still sounds an awful lot like "Good works will save you." But before you decide for sure, let's finish our story.

After the rich young man goes away sad, Jesus tells his disciples, "It is easier for a camel to go through the eye of a needle than for a rich man to enter the Kingdom of God" (Matthew 19:24, NKJV).

These words astonish Jesus' disciples because at the time, not all that different from today, people equated wealth with God's blessings. Upon hearing this, then, the disciples would have thought, "If the people God has blessed can't be part of God's Kingdom, then who can?"

But that's when Jesus says, "With man, this is impossible, but with God all things are possible" (Matthew 19:26). In other words, "You're human. As humans, no matter how hard you try, you're not going to be able follow all the rules. That's impossible." That's also why it's good we don't have to.

Being part of God's Kingdom isn't about what we do; it's about what God's already done through Jesus' life, death, and resurrection. Through *his* good works, we are saved. Through him, all injustices will one day be made right. With him, all things are indeed possible.

That's good news for those of us who, like the rich young man, are perpetual rule followers. We no longer need to keep a mental checklist to ensure we've followed all the rules. Jesus' life, death, and resurrection check off anything we might have missed. We are, as the apostle Paul says, saved by grace through faith (Ephesians 2:8).

And because we are, we're free to do good works—not because they save us but because they're our natural response to God's extraordinary love and grace.

JESUS Talk

1. Would you describe yourself as a rule follower? Why or why not?
2. Before reading this section, how would you have answered the rich young man's question, "What good thing must I do to get eternal life?" How would you answer it now?
3. Why do you think wealth and material possessions are so often equated with God's blessings?
4. In this chapter, Jen makes the case that good works don't save you. Do you agree or disagree? Why?
5. How would Christianity be different if it was about our good works instead of Jesus' good works?
6. What's the difference between doing good works because they save us and doing good works in response to God's extraordinary love and grace? Why do you typically do good works?

> "Tolerance is just accepting people. You don't have to like them. You don't say hateful thing about them. You see them as people. You don't have to love them. [But] I think Jesus loved everyone."
>
> — COLE

23: Did JESUS Teach Tolerance?

When I was in high school, my youth group included one girl who no one really liked. This girl was different than everyone else. She was weird and exceptionally annoying. Much to our credit, we didn't make fun of her... at least not out in the open.

We didn't exclude her either... at least not in obvious ways.

We even put up with her—at least at youth group—but my friends and I never invited her to hang out with us outside of youth group.

In short, we tolerated her.

We even gave ourselves a big pat on the back, convinced that by tolerating her, we were following Jesus' example. The problem is Jesus never taught tolerance. He taught something much more difficult than tolerance: love. In Matthew 22:39, Jesus tells his followers that the second greatest commandment is "Love your neighbor as yourself." In Matthew 5:44, he says, "Love your enemies and pray for those who persecute you." The key word in both of these commandments is *love*. Love does what tolerance cannot.

Tolerance doesn't teach us to respect those who are different than us. It doesn't even teach us to like those who are different than us. It's possible to tolerate someone you actually despise.

Tolerance also doesn't teach us to embrace differences and learn from them. It doesn't teach us to find the inherent dignity and worth of a person that comes from being created in God's image. Tolerance doesn't teach forgiveness or true acceptance. But love does.

What's more, genuine love compels people to change. Just ask the Samaritan woman who Jesus met at the well. This woman was, in every way, an outcast—the person the rest of the town merely tolerated. In fact, we find her at the well at the "sixth hour," which is noon (John 4:6). This is unusual because it's the hottest part of the day. Choosing to go to the well then would be like purposefully choosing to go outside to mow your lawn at noon, when it's 100 degrees out, rather than at 7:00 p.m., when it's only 85 degrees. Since fetching her water at that time of day would have been unpleasant, we assume the woman did this to avoid those who merely tolerated her.

"Jesus taught us to love everyone no matter who they are."

— ISABEL

You see, the well was something of a town meeting spot. It's where all the women came to hang out and hear about what was going on with all their friends and their enemies. It's the place women loved to be... Unless of course, you were the object of the gossip, which this woman certainly was. After all, she'd had five husbands (John 4:18). To make matters worse, she was currently living with someone who wasn't her husband (John 4:18).

If you've ever been gossiped about, you know what this is like—how humiliating it is to hear people whisper about you... only to have the whispering stop the second you're within earshot.

No wonder the woman picked a time to fetch water when she knew she'd be alone.

Except on this one occasion, she isn't. When she arrives at the well, she finds Jesus. Much to this woman's surprise, despite the fact that he clearly knows her story, he's not gossiping about her or looking at her with disdain. He's not staring her down or ignoring her. Instead, he looks at her and asks, "Will you give me a drink?" with a voice filled with compassion (John 4:7).

At the well, Jesus talks to this woman, despite the fact that he's a man and she's a woman and in those days, men didn't talk publicly to a woman unless they were married. Jesus drinks from this woman's cup, despite the fact that he's a Jew and she's a Samaritan and the two groups were sworn enemies who didn't associate with one another. Each time Jesus breaks a social custom, he shows this woman love. Before long, their conversation turns to faith.

Jesus tells this woman about living water. In response, the woman demonstrates she knows the history of her faith by referencing the Old Testament patriarch Jacob. She asks Jesus, "Do you think you're greater than our ancestor Jacob, who gave us this well? How can you offer better water than he and his sons and his animals enjoyed?" (John 4:12).

To this, Jesus essentially tells her, "You bet I'm greater than Jacob. If you drink from this well of his, you'll be thirsty again. But if you drink from *my* well, you'll never thirst" (John 4:13-14).

In response, the woman tells Jesus, "I want some of that so I don't have to keep coming to this well, this place where I'm stared at and routinely made fun of."

That's when Jesus reveals he knows why this woman's the talk of the town. "You have had five husbands and the man you now have is not your husband" (John 4:18).

Although Jesus acknowledges her sordid past, he does not condemn her for it. Instead, he loves her.

Perhaps because he does, the woman realizes that Jesus is a prophet and begins talking to him about the different places people worship. Jesus then teaches her about true worship, telling her, "A time is coming and has now come when the true worshipers will worship the Father in spirit and truth, for they are the kind of worshipers the Father seeks. God is spirit and his worshipers must worship in spirit and in truth" (John 4.23-24).

That's when the light bulb goes off for this woman. She puts together everything Jesus has said.

living water + intimate knowledge about her life that she never told him + an understandable explanation of true worship

For her, this could only add up to one thing. So she says, "I know the Messiah is coming. When he comes, he will explain everything to us" (John 4:25).

Jesus then confirms his identity to this woman, revealing to her that he is the long awaited Messiah of whom she speaks.

At this, the woman returns to her neighbors—the people who for so long have simply tolerated her—and invites them to come see the man who told her everything she'd done. Because of her efforts, many Samaritans from that city believed in Jesus (John 4:39).

For years, this woman's neighbors had merely tolerated her. In the face of their tolerance, she never changed. But after experiencing Jesus' love for one afternoon, the woman changes, radically and completely. Her love for her neighbors then changes her entire town.

Love does what tolerance can't.

As 1 Corinthians 13 says, "Love is patient, love is kind. It does not envy, it does not boast, it is not proud. It does not dishonor others, it is not self-seeking, it is not easily angered, it keeps no record of wrongs. Love does not delight in evil but rejoices with the truth. It always protects, always trusts, always hopes, always perseveres. Love never fails."

Did you hear that?

Love never fails... even when tolerance does.

Love restores people's dignity and worth rather than diminishes it like tolerance so often does.

Love sacrifices, even to the point of death, and it does so because God doesn't just tolerate us. He loves us. As John 3:16 says, "For God so loved the world that he gave his only Son that whoever believes in him may not perish but have eternal life." Can you imagine if that verse instead read, "For God so tolerated the world that he gave his only Son"? It'd be preposterous to make such a sacrifice for people you merely tolerate.

> "Jesus taught that to love one another is why we are on earth. We need to love and help everybody."
>
> — JADE

Thank goodness God does more than that.

Thank goodness God loves us.

May we who follow Jesus have the courage to do likewise—to love others rather than merely tolerate them.

JESUS Talk

1. What's the difference between love and tolerance?
2. Who in your life do you tolerate? Love?
3. For you to love people rather than tolerate them, what would have to change?
4. Which does Jesus do: love you or tolerate you? How do you know?
5. In this chapter, Jen makes the case that Jesus taught love, not tolerance. Do you agree with her? Why or why not?
6. Why's it important that Jesus taught love? Had Jesus merely tolerated people, how would Christianity be different? If Jesus commanded us to merely tolerate people, how would our world be different?

"If you believed that sin was okay, we wouldn't be living the lives Jesus wants us to live. Believing that God forgives our sins is one of the basic parts of being a Christian."

— GARRETT

24: Did JESUS Teach that It's Okay to Sin?

Let me ask you a question: In the last 24 hours, how did you sin?

I'm guessing there's a pretty good chance my question made you uncomfortable. I mean, who wants to talk about sin, much less acknowledge the ways we've sinned ourselves?

I know I don't.

The fact that sin makes me uncomfortable doesn't make it any less real.

On an average day I might not commit HUGE sins. Rest assured, though, I sin each and every day. I snap at my husband. I get jealous over someone or something. I covet—or long for something—that's not mine. I might even tell a few white lies.

Believe me. I know these things are bad.

Even so, sometimes I wonder: If Jesus forgives our sins, then the little ones are okay, aren't they? If Jesus tells us to forgive our brother 77 times—essentially as often as needed—won't he forgive our sins, again and again? (Matthew 18:22) And if Jesus forgives our sins again and again, then is it okay for us to sin?

The answer to this question is found in one of my favorite stories in the Gospels, the story of the adulterous woman, which is told in John 8:1-11.

In this story, Jesus is teaching when all of the sudden, the religious leaders drag in a woman caught in adultery. We assume this woman is naked since she's been caught in adultery, essentially pulled from her bed. The religious leaders probably didn't care enough about her to stop and let her grab some clothes, not when they seem determined to humiliate her.

And make no mistake, this woman would have been humiliated. After all, Jesus' teaching has drawn a crowd of people whose attention is now focused entirely on her.

"Sin is something that goes against God, which is not okay. God forgives us because he has a never-ending love for us."

— KAELA

This woman is also probably frightened. As the religious leaders are quick to remind Jesus, the punishment for adultery is death. According to them, "In the law Moses commanded us to stone such women. What do you say?" (John 8:5).

Now to be clear, the religious leaders have taken a few liberties with the way they've paraphrased this law. According to them, "Moses commanded us to stone such women." According to Moses, "If a man commits adultery with another man's wife—with the wife of his neighbor—both the adulterer and the adulteress are to be put to death" (Leviticus 20:10, emphasis mine).

This begs the question: Where's the man in this story? Why isn't he also standing before Jesus?

Maybe the man set this woman up, essentially framing her so the religious leaders could trap Jesus. Maybe in return, the religious leaders let him go free.

Whatever the reason, the woman is left alone to face the punishment for their crime. Her fear is likely growing by the second, especially when, rather than answer the religious leader's question, Jesus instead begins writing on the ground.

This begs another question. What did Jesus write?

Perhaps Jesus wrote Moses' actual law, a reminder to the religious leaders that they didn't get it quite right when they quoted it back to Jesus. Or maybe Jesus wrote the names of the religious leaders along with a list of their most recent sins—a reminder that they're not all that different from this woman.

Regardless, Jesus' writing doesn't faze the religious leaders, who keep pestering him with questions. Eventually, Jesus stands up and says, "Let anyone among you who is without sin be the first to throw a stone at her" (John 8:7, NRSV).

At these words, I imagine the woman standing there in tears—a combination of relief and embarrassment. I picture the religious leaders with a look of horror on their faces as they slowly realize there's no way they can stone this woman now. I see Jesus suppressing a smirk from the Pharisees before turning to the woman with an unmistakable look of love on his face and asking her, "Has no one condemned you?" (John 8:10).

At this, she responds, "No one, sir" (John 8:11).

Jesus then replies, "Neither do I condemn you" (John 8:11).

It's a moment of sheer grace. As the one person who's never sinned, Jesus could rightfully have condemned this woman. Yet he chooses not to. Rather than stone her like she deserves, Jesus grants this woman mercy. He forgives her and he tells her, "Go and sin no more" (John 8:11, NKJV).

It's that last line that I think gives us our answer to the question, "Did Jesus teach it's okay to sin?"

Clearly, he didn't.

As God, Jesus is holy. He cannot stand sin. So in the face of sin, he challenges people, "Go and sin no more."

His hope for this woman is that she'll never sin again.

Even so, as God, Jesus knows she will.

Sure, she might avoid adultery. How could she not after this powerful encounter with Jesus?

But she'll certainly commit other sins.

That's why I think the order here is important.

Jesus' love and forgiveness isn't conditional upon this woman's ability to "go and sin no more." If it was, Jesus would have said, "*If* you go and sin no more, *then* I won't condemn you."

But that's not what Jesus says. He first offers the woman love, without condemnation. Then he tells her to go and sin no more.

> "Sin is like speeding: Just because you don't get punished every time you do it doesn't mean it's okay to do."
>
> — NOAH

Jesus makes it clear that sin is not okay. But he also reminds this woman—and us—that when we sin, we're forgiven.

In the same way, each time we sin, Jesus offers us his unconditional love and forgiveness. Then he commands us to "go and sin no more."

He invites us to respond to his love with our actions.

In doing so, Jesus shows us that forgiveness isn't a license to sin more. It's a compelling call to change.

JESUS Talk

1. Does talking about sin make you uncomfortable? Why or why not?
2. The moment when Jesus chooses not to condemn the adulterous woman is a moment of sheer grace. What is grace? How are grace and forgiveness related?
3. Jesus forgave the adulterous woman even though we never see her ask for forgiveness. Does this mean we are forgiven—even if we don't ask for forgiveness? Why or why not?
4. How might viewing forgiveness as a license to sin impact your behavior?
5. According to Jen, forgiveness is a compelling call to change. Think about your life. When have you experienced forgiveness? How did that forgiveness change you?
6. In this chapter, Jen makes the case that Jesus doesn't teach that sin is okay. Do you agree or disagree? Why?

"I want to think that one of Jesus' messages is for me to be happy, but I think being a part of his mission is so much better than just me, one person out of seven billion, being happy. Happiness is such a small thing when you compare it to saving the whole world!"

— NICOLE

25: Did JESUS Teach that Faith Leads to Happiness?

What do you want to be when you grow up?

Maybe you want to be a doctor, a lawyer, or a journalist. Or maybe you want to be a teacher or an engineer. Or perhaps you want to own your own business.

Regardless of what job you want to have, I'm guessing what you want most is to be happy.

Maybe that's even what the people around you want most for you.

I mean, it's what Jesus wants for you, isn't it? Didn't Jesus even say, "Blessed are those who are happy"?

No.

Jesus never uttered those words... or any like them. No matter how many times you search Jesus' words for promises of happiness, you won't find them. Regardless of how many times you hope Jesus will promise his followers an easy life, he doesn't. Instead, just before his death, Jesus reminds his followers, "In this world you will have trouble" (John 16:33).

Jesus doesn't specify what kind of trouble we'll have. He just lets us know it's coming.

Maybe you'll fight with your siblings, friends, and parents. You might get cut from the team or play you really want to be part of, or get dumped by your significant other. Maybe you'll fail tests or disappoint people. Eventually, you may even lose a job or your house. At some point in your life, people you love will die.

Jesus is right.

In this world, you will have trouble, even if you're his follower, or perhaps *especially* if you're a follower of Jesus. After all, while the aforementioned "troubles" are ones that *all* people will face, Jesus also mentions a few hardships specific to his followers. In Luke 9:23 (NSRVA), he says, "If any want to become my followers, let them deny themselves and take up their cross daily and follow me." Far from promising his followers a life of happiness and ease, Jesus promises us a life of suffering and hardship.

To be clear, I don't think Jesus' ultimate goal is for us to be miserable. I just think he wants to give us a reality check, to ensure we know what we're getting into as his followers.

In the Kingdom of God, everything will be reversed, so much so that "the last will be first, and the first will be last" (Matthew 20:16). Part of that reversal is Jesus' definition of greatness. In his words, "Whoever wishes to be great among you must be your servant" (Matthew 20:26, NSRVA).

In this upside down Kingdom of God, Jesus' ultimate goal is far bigger than any individual's happiness, including ours. It's saving the world. As Jesus tells the tax collector Zacchaeus, "The Son of Man came to seek and to save the lost" (Luke 19:10).

As Jesus' followers, we get to be part of this mission—not because Jesus can't do it without us, but because he loves us. Jesus knows sharing in his mission will make for the best life possible. He's so sure about this that in John 10:10 he says, "The thief comes only to steal and kill and destroy; I have come that they may have life, and have it to the full."

"My own personal happiness is not the ultimate goal; spreading God's love and message is."

— GABE

Choosing to be part of Jesus' mission to seek out and save the lost might mean going places you never planned or doing things you never expected or wanted to do. It might even mean upsetting your parents or your friends. In short, being a follower of Jesus won't be easy and it won't guarantee you happiness. Jesus never promises that.

What Jesus promises is his peace and ultimate victory. In the same verse where he tells us, "In this world you will have trouble," he also says, "I have told you these things, so that in me you may have peace. But take heart! I have overcome the world" (John 16:33).

As followers of Jesus, we won't be immune to trouble, hard things, or suffering but we can take heart, knowing that Jesus has overcome the world.

Now, that may not be the kind of "happy" life you envision for yourself.

What Jesus wants for you is something far harder than that... and far better.

JESUS Talk

1. Answer the question at the start of this chapter: "What do you want to be when you grow up?" Why?
2. Thus far in your life, what kind of trouble have you experienced?
3. According to Jen, "Jesus' ultimate goal is far bigger than any individual's happiness." To you, what does this mean? Do you agree or disagree with this? Why?
4. How are you currently participating in Jesus' mission to seek and save the lost?
5. How willing are you to follow Jesus even if doing so leads to conflict with people like your parents? Why?
6. In the midst of the troubles of this world, when have you experienced Jesus' peace?
7. How has Jesus overcome the world?
8. In this chapter, Jen argues that Jesus didn't teach that happiness is our ultimate goal. Do you agree or disagree? Why?

"If you are able to help yourself, then you just focus on yourself and meeting your own needs. But if others help you, then you are forced to be vulnerable and learn the value of community."

— MELODY

26: Did JESUS Teach Self-Help?

If you know people who've been on a mission trip, chances are, you've heard them say something like, "I got so much more out of that experience than I gave."

Maybe you've even said something similar after returning from a mission trip. I know I have. I can remember standing at mission trip celebrations, sharing our experience with the congregation, and sobbing, "I thought I was going to help others but they helped me so much more!" There's just something about serving others that makes us feel good, that makes us feel fulfilled.

As mission trips teach us, sometimes the best way to help ourselves is by helping others. Is it any wonder then that Jesus was constantly telling his followers to serve others?

According to him, we're supposed to feed the hungry, give drinks to the thirsty, welcome the stranger, clothe the naked, care for the sick, and visit those in prison—just to name a few (Matthew 25:35).

Sure, doing these things benefits the recipient. They're less hungry, thirsty, and lonely. It also makes the Kingdom of God more of a present day reality here on earth. But above and beyond those two things, I think Jesus knew that helping others would also benefit us.

Jesus was no Dr. Phil. When someone needed help, Jesus didn't give them 10 handy-dandy steps so that they could help themselves. Instead, he connected them to another person, knowing that most often our needs are met in community. What one person lacks, another person has.

In truth, this is hard.

Oh—it's not hard to help others. That part is easy. After all, as we've already established, that makes us feel good.

What's hard is asking others to help us. We'd much rather help ourselves than be dependent on someone else for help. It's the American way.

Trust me, I know.

I was an engineering major in college. As part of this, I had to take a lot of math. One of my least favorite classes ever was multivariable calculus. I struggled with this class, day in and day out. I'd do all the homework and study my butt off but inevitably, I'd still fail our tests and quizzes. As much as I tried to make sense of it, I just couldn't.

You know what was almost as hard for me as multivariable calculus?

Asking for help with multivariable calculus.

> "Helping others does wonders for your health, faith, and happiness, so it can bring about healing in those aspects."
>
> — COOPER

Asking someone for help meant admitting my weakness. It meant saying, "I can't do this by myself." Doing that made me feel like a failure, especially in a culture that applauds intelligence and our ability to figure things out on our own.

Eventually, though, I realized there was a very real possibility that without help, I'd fail the class. So I hired a tutor, who explained the concepts in a way that finally made sense to me. With his help, I no longer toiled for hours only to still get my homework wrong and fail the tests. My worry about this class lessened and my life improved drastically. So did my grade. That never would have happened had I continued trying to go it alone.

The same is true of so many things in life.

Life is better when we courageously admit we need help, whether it's with a class or something even more serious than that.

What's more, when we have the courage to admit when we need help, we give others the opportunity to serve us. And as anyone who's ever gone a mission trip knows, then they, too, are blessed.

"The Kingdom of God is one big kingdom, not many little kingdoms. We are all intertwined and therefore, we are dependent on each other."

— PAT

In Jesus' Kingdom, it's not every man for himself. It's every person for each other. It's about being able to ask others for help just as much as being willing to help others. It's about interdependence, not independence.

On multiple occasions, Jesus told his disciples, "Whoever finds his life will lose it, and whoever loses his life for my sake will find it" (Matthew 10:39). He said this on the heels of telling his disciples to pick up their crosses and follow him. As a result, we so often interpret this as Jesus saying, "Don't worry if you die because by believing in me, you'll go to heaven and gain eternal life."

That's true, but I wonder if these words might also mean that when we shift our focus from ourselves to others, we gain something in the here and now: health and wholeness.

God the Father knew we couldn't save ourselves. That's why he sent Jesus.

Jesus knew we couldn't even effectively help ourselves. But we can help each other... and in so doing, we just might discover that we've been helped too.

JESUS Talk

1. Describe a time when, on a mission trip or service project, you gained far more than you gave.
2. In what ways does serving others help those being served? Those who are serving?
3. Jesus could have given people 10 handy-dandy ways to help themselves. Why do you think he didn't?
4. According to Jen, most often our needs are met in community. Think about you church community. How has it met your needs? The needs of others?
5. Why is interdependence important in the Kingdom of God?
6. How might helping others bring about our own healing?
7. After reading this chapter, do you think Jesus taught self-help? Why or why not?

"Jesus chose to die for our sins and allow us to make mistakes today."
— EVAN

27: Did **Jesus** Teach that Success Means Never Failing?

I don't like to fail.

I'm guessing you don't either.

I still remember the time when, during a piano recital, I forgot my piece and burst into tears in front of several hundred people.

Did I mention I was only 6?

I remember getting a B in 7th grade gym because I couldn't hit the soccer ball with my head. It was the only B I got on my report card that year.

I remember striking out EVERY TIME I was at bat during my softball games in junior high. I'll never understand why they even let me be on the team.

I remember getting cut from the volleyball team as a freshman in high school.

I remember the time in sophomore English when my teacher told me—in front of my peers—that I didn't deserve to be ranked first in my class.

I remember the C- I got on an AP English paper on *Pride and*

Prejudice, along with the comment from that same English teacher: "This paper never really got off the ground."

Each failure devastated me because I'd learned that success meant never failing.

I was so convinced of this that I honestly thought people's love for me was contingent on my ability to not fail. I just knew my parents would love me less if I stopped getting straight As. Deep down, I think I even believed this was true of Jesus.

I was so wrong.

Far from being repelled by failure, Jesus embraces it.

Just look at how he responds to his BFF, Peter.

Peter is a guy who constantly sticks his foot in his mouth, acting and speaking before thinking things through. He's the guy who sinks while attempting to walk on water (Matthew 14:30). He constantly misunderstands Jesus—so much so that Jesus once calls him Satan (Matthew 16:23). On the night Jesus is arrested, Peter takes out his sword and cuts a guy's ear off (which Jesus then heals—John 18:10). After Jesus is arrested, Peter denies him not once, not twice, but three times.

The first time he denies Jesus, Peter is sitting in a courtyard, trying his darnedest to catch a glimpse of Jesus during his trial in order to show his support. While there, a servant girl comes up to him and says, "You also were with Jesus of Galilee." In response, Peter cries, "I don't know what you're talking about" (Matthew 26:69-70).

Undeterred, Peter carries on, making his way to the gate, hoping to find out what's going on with Jesus. Again, someone recognizes him and says, "This fellow was with Jesus of Nazareth." Rather than confirm his identity, Peter yells, "I don't know the man!" (Matthew 26:72).

Still, Peter refuses to leave, to abandon Jesus like the rest of his so-called friends have done. Soon, someone else recognizes him. "Surely you are one of them; your accent gives you away" (Matthew 26:73).

Perhaps fearing he'll be arrested and even killed, Peter begins calling down curses on himself. He swears, "I don't know the man!" (Matthew 26:74).

In the hours when Jesus most needs a friend, Peter fails him. He denies he even knows Jesus.

Despite these failures, this is the man Jesus chooses to be his number one. This is the man Jesus wants to lead his church. This is the man Jesus calls the "rock"—even though as God, he knows Peter's going to let him down (Matthew 16:18).

As his relationship with Peter demonstrates, Jesus doesn't measure success according to how seldom a person fails. He understands we learn from failures. Had Peter not sunk when he tried to walk on water, would he have ever learned to depend on him? Would he have ever been able to confidently call Jesus the "Christ, the Son of the living God" (Matthew 16:16)?

"Jesus taught us that we don't need to be perfect to reach heaven."

— ANNIE

Rather than eliminate people because of their failures, Jesus looks past our failures and sees our potential, just like he does with Peter.

Three times Peter denies Jesus. But after Jesus rises from the dead, he finds Peter. Three times he asks Peter if he loves him. Each time Peter says he does. Each time, Jesus tells him, "Feed my Lambs" (John 21:15-17). In essence, Jesus says, "Peter, I'm not done with you. Your failures haven't eliminated you from leadership. So come on. We've got work to do."

You see, according to Jesus, success isn't measured by the absence of failures. Success is measured by our faithfulness to the one who redeems our failures.

JESUS Talk

1. Describe a time you failed. Why do you think you can remember your failures so vividly?
2. Given Peter's extensive list of failures, would he be qualified to be a leader in your church? Why or why not? Does Jesus' willingness to give him a position of leadership surprise you? Why or why not?
3. How do Peter's failures contribute to his ability to call Jesus the "Christ, the Son of the living God"?
4. How have your failures shaped how you see Jesus? Impacted your relationship with him?
5. Despite your failures, what potential do you think Jesus sees in you? Why?
6. In this chapter, Jen argues that Jesus didn't teach that success is the absence of failure. Do you agree or disagree? Why?
7. According to Jen, "Success is measured by our faithfulness to the one who redeems our failures." How are you being faithful to Jesus in spite of your failures? How has Jesus redeemed your failures?

Section Six

Did JESUS Sin?

"All who sin fall short of the glory of God. If you sin, you can't get into heaven. It would make no sense for Jesus to have sinned and even get into heaven, let alone be the sacrifice for all of us. If Jesus sinned, it would have defeated the purpose of him coming. He was our example of how we should live."

— ADAM

28: Does It Really Matter Whether or Not JESUS Sinned?

Think about your average Friday. In the course of your day, how many temptations do you face?

During an average Friday you're in school, you might be tempted to cheat on a test, copy a friend's homework, plagiarize part of your English paper, or talk about that weird kid behind his back. When you get home, you might be tempted to lie to your parents about how you did on your test or about your weekend plans. Later that night, you might be tempted to drink at your friend's house or to sneak home a few minutes after your curfew since you know your parents will be sound asleep.

Every day, we all encounter numerous temptations. Since he was fully human, Jesus did too.

Matthew 4 tells us about the most famous series of temptations Jesus encountered, a time during which the Spirit led Jesus into the desert specifically to be tempted (Matthew 4:1). While in the desert, Jesus participates in the ancient spiritual discipline of fasting—going without food in order to draw closer to God by using the time you'd normally spend eating to pray. He fasts for 40 days and nights.

For several years, I've fasted with those in my youth ministry during World Vision's 30 Hour Famine. During this event, we go without food for 30 hours in order to "taste" hunger so that we can better understand and empathize with those throughout the world who are hungry. As we do, we raise money for those who are suffering from hunger around the world.

Maybe you've also participated in the 30 Hour Famine. If you have, you know how hungry you are by the end of it. If you haven't, let me try to describe it for you.

The last few hours of the Famine are absolutely brutal.

Your stomach rumbles.

Your head hurts.

You're exhausted because you haven't eaten anything.

You're cranky, snapping at the littlest things.

You're trying desperately NOT to think about food, because it only makes you more hungry. But since you haven't eaten in 30 hours, food is the only thing you can think of.

By the time you eat your first meal, you feel like you could devour everything in sight because you're hungrier than you've ever been before.

Knowing how hungry I am at the end of a 30-hour fast, I cannot even begin to imagine how hungry Jesus must have been after 40 DAYS of fasting. No wonder the devil chooses to tempt Jesus first with food, telling him, "If you are the son of God, tell these stones to become bread" (Matthew 4:3).

Despite his hunger, Jesus refuses to fall for the devil's temptation. He says, "It is written: 'Man shall not live on bread alone, but on every word that comes from the mouth of God'" (Matthew 4:4).

Not one to give up, the devil tries again. He takes Jesus to the city and dares him to throw himself off the temple in order to see if God will send his angels to save him. Again, Jesus refuses, relying on Scripture to resist the temptation.

The devil then tempts Jesus a third time by taking him to the top of a tall mountain, showing him all the kingdoms of the world, and promising to give them to him if Jesus will simply bow down and worship him. Once again, Jesus resists, emphatically telling the devil, "It is written, 'Worship the Lord your God and serve him only'" (Matthew 4:10).

With this, the devil leaves.

"He was the perfect person. He never did anything wrong."

— MEGAN

Now, in some ways, it's easy to ignore the importance of this story. I mean, sure Jesus was tempted. But so are we. What's the big deal?

It's precisely because both we and Jesus are tempted that this story matters. Since Jesus was tempted, he can relate to us. But unlike us, Jesus never gave into his temptations. He NEVER sinned. In this way, he's clearly unlike us. Because Jesus is both like us and unlike us, he can serve as our high priest—the go-between for us and God. That's what the author of Hebrews means when he says, "We do not have a high priest who is unable to empathize with our weaknesses, but we have one who has been tempted in every way, just as we are, yet he did not sin" (Hebrews 4:15).

That's important.

Had Jesus given into any of these or other temptations, then like us, he'd be a sinner. As a sinner, Jesus would be unfit to be our Savior. How could he be when he himself would have needed a Savior?

But as someone who was tempted and never sinned, Jesus is instead the perfect high priest. Since he understands us, he can represent us to God. Since the punishment for sin is death, Jesus is literally the only person who doesn't deserve to die. As a result, he can die in our place. Since Jesus never needed forgiveness, he's in the unique position to forgive our sins once and for all.

"Although sinless, Jesus still had struggles like us."

— CHLOE

That's good news since eventually, unlike Jesus, you and I will actually give in to something that tempts us. We'll cross over the line from being tempted to sinning. When we do, we'll need a Savior.

Thankfully, in Jesus—the one who was tempted yet never sinned— we have one.

JESUS Talk

1. What are some of the temptations you commonly face?
2. How does having faced temptations allow Jesus to sympathize with our weaknesses?
3. Why would sin make Jesus unfit to be our Savior?
4. After reading this chapter, how would you answer the question, "Does it really matter whether or not Jesus sinned?" Why?

"Jesus was a child. All children make mistakes. Even if it's not written in the Bible, there's got to be something he did that wasn't 100% morally correct or spiritually correct. Whether it was at age of two or 15. He was a guy, small child, teenager. Those are all really big times to sin."

— CONNOR

29: Disobedient JESUS?

It's much easier for me to picture Jesus as an adult than as a child. Maybe this is because the Gospels—the four eyewitness accounts of Jesus' life, teaching, death, and resurrection—provide us with plenty of stories about Jesus that help us envision what his life was like as an adult. Artists' depictions of these stories further bring them to life.

That's not the case with the boy Jesus, who the Gospels tell us surprisingly little about. From the Gospels, we know...

1. A little about Jesus' birth
2. That Jesus' parents followed Jewish custom and named him when he was circumcised, eight days after his birth
3. That Jesus was presented at the temple
4. That eventually some Magi came and worshiped Jesus
5. That the Magi's visit prompted King Herod to unleash his horror and massacre the infants and that that prompted Jesus and his family to flee to Egypt in order to avoid being killed by King Herod
6. And that eventually, Jesus' family returned to Nazareth

That's it. We know six things about Jesus' early life. Then, nothing.

We have no record of Jesus' first word, tooth, or step. We have no idea what he was like as a toddler.

We also have no idea what he was like as a kid. Did he enjoy school? What was his favorite subject? Who did he hang out with? Did he get along with his brothers and sisters? Did he perform miracles? Did he know, even then, that he was God?

Then suddenly, when Jesus is 12, we get a brief glimpse of him in Luke 2:41-52.

In this story, Jesus and his family travel to Jerusalem to celebrate Passover. Afterward, his family returns to Nazareth. A day into the journey, his parents realize Jesus is nowhere to be found.

That's right. Mary and Joseph lose Jesus. Now, as a youth pastor, I know the importance of taking a headcount whenever our group gets into a van to go somewhere. Knowing this, it's almost incomprehensible to me that Mary and Joseph could LOSE their son. How hard could it have been for them to double check that the son of God was actually with them when they left Jerusalem?

Maybe harder than you think.

You see, Jesus' family wasn't traveling alone. Instead, they were traveling with a caravan of family and friends—all returning home after the Passover celebration. In such a caravan, it wouldn't have been unusual for teens to separate from their parents in order to walk with their friends.

I'm sure you can relate. Wouldn't you rather ride in a car with your friends than your parents?

In light of this, Jesus' parents would have had no reason to worry. They'd have assumed Jesus was with his friends and that when they stopped for food and rest, they'd find him.

But that's not what happens.

When they stop to rest, Jesus isn't there.

Frantic with worry, Mary and Joseph return to Jerusalem, which mind you, is a big city. They retrace their steps and search for Jesus everywhere they can think of, their worry likely increasing each minute they go without finding Jesus.

Left with no other place to turn, after three days Mary and Joseph finally go to the temple, perhaps in order to pray for the return of their son.

That's what I'd do. In those moments when I'm left with nowhere else to turn, I go to church, desperately searching for God.

Much to their surprise, when they get to the temple, Mary and Joseph find Jesus. Oblivious to their worry, Jesus is deep in conversation with the rabbis.

Upon seeing this, Mary is of course relieved.

Her relief quickly turns to anger, as she asks Jesus, "Son, why have you treated us like this? Your father and I have been anxiously searching for you" (Luke 2:48).

To me, that line just doesn't do this scene justice.

Picture those times in your life when you've caused your parents to worry. Whenever I caused my parents worry, their response was not a calm question. It was words screamed in anger, frustration, and fury that left no doubt I was in trouble.

That's how I picture Mary here.

And yet, Jesus seems clueless. He tells her, "Did you not know that I must be in my Father's house?" (Luke 2:49, ESV).

Now, if I said that to my mom, I think she'd accuse me of being disrespectful, of talking back to her. In fact, we often think Jesus is being disobedient here because we read his response through the lens of the fourth commandment: "Honor your father and mother, so that your days may be long in the land that the Lord your God is giving you" (Exodus 20:12, ESV).

At first glance, it seems that by staying behind in Jerusalem, Jesus disobeyed and in so doing, dishonored his parents who clearly expected him to go back to Nazareth with them. But then consider Jesus' words to Mary: "Did you not know that I must be in my Father's house?" For Jesus, "Father's house" is more than just a metaphor. It's not just a different way of referring to the synagogue. It's a way of referring to his actual Father—God—whose house, according to Jewish custom, is in fact the temple. Far from disobeying or dishonoring his mother and father by staying behind in the Jerusalem temple, Jesus is actually honoring his true Father, God.

The problem is Mary and Joseph don't understand what Jesus is saying. Even though they've been visited by an angel, they still don't get who they're raising. When Jesus tells them he's in his Father's house, they're oblivious to the fact that he's saying God is his actual Father.

Again, this isn't an act of disobedience. It's a simple miscommunication or perhaps even more accurately, a misunderstanding.

After Mary and Joseph find Jesus, he returns with them to Nazareth. Scripture tells us outright that Jesus is "obedient to them," growing in "wisdom and in years, in divine and human favor" (Luke 2:51-52, NRSVA).

The one thing the Bible tells us about teenage Jesus is that he's obedient. During the time when many of us are *most* rebellious, Jesus remains obedient. He remains sinless. In some ways, it's even harder for me to picture that than it is for me to imagine Jesus as a child.

Yet, just because it's hard to picture doesn't make it any less true. According to Scripture, Jesus never sinned—not even as a child or teenager.

JESUS Talk

1. How easy or difficult is it for you to picture Jesus as a child? A teenager? Why?
2. Why do you think Scripture includes so little information about Jesus as a child?
3. According to Jen, "By staying behind in the Jerusalem temple, Jesus is actually honoring his true Father, God." How?
4. At what point do you think Mary and Joseph finally began understanding who Jesus was? Why?
5. Why do you think Scripture explicitly tells us that Jesus remained obedient to his parents during his teenage years?
6. Jen makes the case in this chapter that when Jesus stayed behind in the Jerusalem temple, he didn't sin. Do you agree or disagree? Why?

"I know in the Bible, Jesus went through the temple and flipped tables and broke things. I don't know if that'd be considered a sin."

— ISAAC

30: Ticked Off JESUS?

At a fairly young age, my parents taught me it was inappropriate to yell or throw things in public, even when you're angry. At the same time, I remember learning that emotions aren't sinful. This confused me. Is anger a sin or isn't it?

As I got older, people tried to address my confusion by saying things like, "Emotions aren't sinful, but how you respond to them can be."

Oh, yeah. Because that makes complete sense.

My confusion only increased after learning about Jesus' very public hissy fit, one that came complete with yelling and throwing things. During it, he goes into the temple and flips out. According to Matthew, he basically ransacks the place, overturning the tables of the money changers (Matthew 21:12). John even has him making a whip to drive the money changers out (John 2:15).

Now, we might be able to excuse Jesus flipping over a few tables, but surely making a whip crosses a line, doesn't it? Surely that's a pretty clear-cut sin, isn't it?

Well, let's investigate this a bit more.

First of all, where is Jesus when this whole event takes place?

Most of us would say he's in the temple. In actuality, Scripture tells us this scene takes place in the "temple area." That might seem like a minor distinction, but in reality, it's an important one.

The temple area was the first part of the temple people entered. It housed all the businesses of the temple. It was where people could buy and sell the animals needed to make the ritual sacrifices required for the forgiveness of sin. This was also the only part of the temple where anyone who wasn't Jewish could worship God and gather for prayer. Between the temple area and the rest of the temple there was essentially a big "Keep Out" sign, forbidding everyone who wasn't Jewish to enter.

The temple was a holy place. It wouldn't be a place for merchants. You picture Jesus being this calm, serene person with a beard. For him to go through and tear down things like that— that's just not how you picture Jesus."

— HANNAH

To translate this into modern times, imagine that to get into your church's worship space, you have to walk through a giant hall. In this hall there are all kinds of people selling you stuff for worship. There's someone selling Bibles, another selling hymnals, and another selling prayer beads. There's even a person selling food. The prices for each of these things is sky high—you know you could buy a Bible for half the price on Amazon. Yet, you also believe these things are necessary for worship. So you make your purchases and keep walking towards the worship space. But when you get to the worship space, there's a giant sign that says, "Reserved for those with PhDs in religion or theology." The doors are guarded by two very big, scary bouncers. With no way through, you're left with no choice but to return to the hall and worship there—with the other riffraff who don't have PhDs. You try to do so, but let's face it. You're constantly distracted by people yelling, "Bibles here!" "Get your coffee here!"

That's essentially what Jesus finds in his Father's house. It's so distressing to him that he gets angry, and rightfully so.

Now, I'll admit. Even that's still hard to comprehend.

So let me try to explain this another way. Imagine your grandparents have just died. After the funeral, your family goes to their house in order to divide up their possessions. One minute you're sitting there, calmly talking through a shroud of grief. The next, everyone is running to grab the things they want. There's no order, only complete and utter chaos. To you, it feels like vultures are descending, eagerly gobbling up the remnants of your grandparents' lives. As you watch the scene unfold, you feel as though your grandparents' house is being ransacked, like people care far more about their stuff than their lives. It feels disrespectful, so much so that you want to hurl... or make a whip and drive your family out of your grandparents' house in order to preserve their memory and dignity.

That's essentially what Jesus finds when he walks into the temple: People disrespecting and dishonoring his own father's house. This is so disturbing to Jesus that he does what he has to do. As they say, drastic times call for drastic measures.

What Jesus does isn't a sin. Rather than break the law, he actually upholds it. By driving out the money changers, he insures that only God the Father is being worshiped, that there are no idols in his Father's house.

What's more, by driving out the money changers, Jesus does something even more important here. To understand what that is, you have to look at Jesus' words. After driving the money changers out, Jesus tells them,

> *"My house will be called a house of prayer **for all nations** but you have made it a den of robbers" (Mark 11:17).*

This is actually a quote from the Old Testament prophet Isaiah, a passage that essentially gave Gentiles the right to worship in the temple area.

By quoting it here, Jesus is sending everyone a powerful message that he has come, not just for the Jews but for ALL people; that because of him, the temple that was once ONLY for the Jews is now for everyone; that through him ALL people have access to God.

Far from sinning, by driving out the money changers in the temple, Jesus is actually undoing a grave injustice—an injustice, I might add, that would have kept you and I out of the temple along with the rest of the Gentiles. Through Jesus' actions here and on the cross, he changes the "Keep Out" sign that once separated the temple area from the rest of the temple to one that says, "Welcome All."

Gentiles or Jews.

Slaves or free.

Wealthy or poor.

Jocks or geeks.

Popular kids or misfits.

Through Jesus, all are welcome in the temple, in the church, and in the Kingdom of God.

JESUS Talk

1. Why is it right—or even just—for Jesus to have been angry about what was happening in the temple?
2. How do Jesus' actions in the temple uphold the law?
3. Jesus' actions in the temple show he's come for ALL people. Even so, who do we sometimes try to exclude from his Kingdom? Why?
4. Jesus gives all people access to God. How?
5. Before reading this chapter, did you think Jesus' actions in the temple were sinful? Why or why not? Do you now? Why or why not?

"Jesus was not exactly a rule follower. He kind of had a tendency to disregard secular rules and things."

— ROBBIE

31: Rebel **JESUS**?

As a Christian, you've probably been told at least once…

Don't smoke.
Don't drink.
Don't have sex until after you're married.

If you've done any of these things, you've likely been labeled a sinner. You might also have been labeled a *rebel,* someone who defiantly goes against the rules.

Sometimes Jesus is also called a *rebel,* since he seemed to reject many of the rules he was expected to follow as a faithful Jew. Take for example, the third commandment: "Remember the Sabbath day by keeping it holy" (Exodus 20:8). Today, when we hear this commandment we usually translate it: "Go to church."

In Jesus' day, however, religious teachers said there were 39 activities you couldn't do on the Sabbath.[2] If you did any one of these 39 things, you broke the third commandment. Among other things, you couldn't work on the Sabbath, which was supposed to be a day of rest, a day of trusting in God's provision. Since you weren't allowed to work on the Sabbath, you also couldn't harvest food on the Sabbath. Doing so would have been work for you and any

---

2. Timothy Keller, *Jesus the King* (Riverhead, 2011), 40.

animals used to harvest your food.

As a good and faithful Jew, Jesus knows this. Yet one day, while Jesus and his disciples are walking along a grain field, they help themselves to some grain.

Unfortunately, the Pharisees—religious leaders who Jesus often butts heads with—catch them in the act, saying, "Look, why are they doing what is unlawful on the Sabbath?" (Mark 2:24).

In response, Jesus says, "The Sabbath was made for man, not man for the Sabbath. So the Son of Man is Lord even of the Sabbath."

Say what?

Essentially, Jesus is telling the Pharisees, "Who are you to tell me what I can and can't do on the Sabbath? You didn't create it. I did."

In other words, Jesus *is* the Sabbath. True rest is found in him— not from taking a day off of work (though that's good too!). Jesus reminds us of this when he tell us, "Come to me, all you who are weary and burdened, and I will give you rest" (Matthew 11:28).

Though the Bible doesn't tell us how the Pharisees react to Jesus' words, I imagine they're pretty upset, especially since Jesus' disregard for their rules continues. The very next chapter of Mark tells of another instance when Jesus does something he's not supposed to on the Sabbath: He heals a man.

In Mark 3:1, Jesus walks into the local synagogue and sees a man with a shriveled hand. This man's visible deformity would have made him an outcast, like the kid at your school who everyone makes fun of or the person who, because he looks different from everyone else, scares you.

This man's life is hard—harder still because his deformity likely prevents him from working. Without work, he can't provide food for himself or his family.

Despite his hard life, this man shows up at the synagogue to worship God. There, he meets Jesus, who does a bit of show and tell with him, parading him in front of everyone—including the Pharisees, who are still ticked at him for all the other ways he's disregarded their rules about the Sabbath. Jesus then asks them, "Which is lawful on the Sabbath: to do good or to do evil, to save life or to kill?" (Mark 3:4).

You might translate Jesus' words like this: "You've become so obsessed with the RULES that you've forgotten why the Sabbath exists in the first place—to provide people with rest and to fix what's broken. Since your laws aren't doing that, I will."

With that, Jesus heals the man's hand. Scripture tells us it's "completely restored" (Mark 3:5). In reality, Jesus restores far more than the man's hand. He restores his life. By healing the man's hand, he gives him a way to work and provide for himself and his family. He gives the man back his dignity.

"Jesus is God. He has that authority to break whatever rules he wants."

— COLLEEN

By healing this man's hand, Jesus does exactly what the Sabbath is supposed to do: heal what's broken.

So there you have it. In order to heal what's broken, Jesus breaks some of the rules created by the religious leaders to help people remember the Sabbath day. But does that make him a sinner?

To answer that, you've got to go back to Jesus' own words.

"The Son of Man is Lord even of the Sabbath."

To be Lord over something means you have authority or control over it. Ultimately, it's Jesus—NOT the religious leaders—who has authority and control over the Sabbath. While Jesus broke some of the rules set by the religious leaders, he did so because they were as imperfect as the people who created them.

"Jesus wasn't afraid to go against the norm; against what society wants you to do. That takes strength."

— ELISE

That's not the case with God's law, which is as perfectly just as he is, designed to right injustices and fix what's broken in the world around us.

Jesus kept that law. He also reminded us that he *is* the law, the one who will heal all that's broken.

JESUS Talk

1. When, if ever, have you been called a rebel?
2. Is rebelling against something always a sin? Why or why not?
3. True rest is found in Jesus. How?
4. The Sabbath is supposed to heal what's broken. How does that compare to your understanding of the Sabbath?
5. To you, what does it mean that Jesus is "Lord over the Sabbath"?

32: Do the Winners Write History?

Ever since my parents took me to Washington, DC, in the third grade, American history has fascinated me. Not surprisingly, one of my favorite classes in high school was AP US History. I loved learning the history of our country and was particularly fascinated by the Revolutionary War.

According to our American history books, the story of the Revolutionary War is pretty clear cut: The British were the bad guys and the Revolutionists were the good guys. The bravery of the Revolutionists made it possible for them to overcome seemingly insurmountable odds in order to emerge victorious over the Queen's army. They secured our freedom with no help from anyone else.

Recently, though, I started watching AMC's *Turn*, which also tells the story of the Revolutionary War. Much to my surprise, however, the story told in *Turn* is quite different than the one I remember learning in history. In it, the Revolutionists are not always the clear-cut good guys. Like the British troops they, too, hang people and punish civilians who are not on their side. What's more, they don't defeat the British alone—they have help from the French, who essentially use us to fight a proxy war against England. *Turn* even makes people like Benedict Arnold—the man I grew up believing was a traitor—seem complicated rather than one-dimensional, as though he might actually have had good reasons for betraying America. In fact, *Turn* makes it seem like General Washington—

the man who according to our history books did no wrong—first betrayed Arnold, passing him over for promotions he deserved because of the victories he won for the Revolutionists.

You could argue that because *Turn* is made for TV, it takes some liberties with how it tells the story of the Revolutionary War. Still, as I've watched it, I've found myself wondering how accurate the history book I read in AP US History actually was. After all, don't the winners write history? If that's true, then it's quite possible that the Revolutionary War was far more complicated than I was led to believe in class.

If it's true that the winners write history, shouldn't we also question Scripture's account of Jesus and in particular, his sinlessness? I mean, the four Gospels—the books that tell of Jesus' life, death, and resurrection—weren't written by impartial people. Two of them were written by Jesus' apostles. The other two were written by people who clearly loved and respected Jesus. Might they have conveniently left out Jesus' sins simply to make him look good?

To answer this, let's consider some of the facts.

First, in contrast to when you read an American history textbook, the people in the Gospels—including Jesus—are complex. Here's what I mean by this: Read an American history textbook's account of the Revolutionary War and you'll learn that Benedict Arnold was, in fact, a traitor. Its accounts of Benedict Arnold leave no room for discussion. He was a bad man who did a horrible thing by betraying those he swore to protect.

In contrast, when you read the four Gospels—Matthew, Mark, Luke, and John—you'll notice that Jesus' friends each portray him differently. They share things about Jesus that, like we've seen in this section, make him look less than perfect. As we've seen in **Section 6: Did Jesus Sin?**, they tell the story of Jesus' temptation, of his leaving his parents as a young boy in order to hang out with his Heavenly

Father at the temple, and of his using a whip to drive people from the temple. The fact that these things are found in the Gospels actually makes them more trustworthy. I mean, if the Gospel writers had left out Jesus' sins, wouldn't they have eliminated *anything* that might cause people to question his sinlessness?

It's also important to consider who wrote the Gospels and what their purpose in writing the Gospels was. Two of the Gospels were written by Jesus' apostles: Matthew and John. Matthew wrote his book to the Jewish people in order to show them that Jesus was the long-awaited Messiah. John openly shares his purpose for writing: "That you may believe that Jesus is the Christ, the Son of God, and that by believing you may have life in his name" (John 20:31). Sure, these guys had agendas for writing their accounts of Jesus' life, but they were open about them.

The other two Gospels were written by Luke and Mark. Luke was a Gentile, a Greek physician who traveled with the Apostle Paul during some of his missionary journeys. Non-Christian historians tend to accept Luke's account of Jesus as accurate, partly due to the amount of verifiable details he includes.

In many ways, though, it's Mark that's the most interesting Gospel for us to consider. We think that John Mark—a close friend of the Apostle Peter—wrote this book. Since Mark explains Jewish customs and translates Aramaic words, we're pretty sure he wrote this book to non-Jewish believers in Rome. Throughout his Gospel, Mark emphasizes Jesus' suffering, as well as the connection between suffering and following Jesus. As a result, his purpose in writing this Gospel was probably to encourage those believers in Rome who were facing persecution and even being put to death for their faith.

To me, Mark's Gospel is the best evidence we have that Jesus' sinlessness isn't merely a case of history being written by the winners. You see, for that to happen, the story has to be written by the winners. But that's not the case with the Gospels.

Matthew, Mark, Luke, and John all tell the story of their leader's excruciating execution on a cross. Sure, Jesus rose from the dead. But at the time Matthew, Mark, Luke, and John wrote their Gospels, it sure didn't look like Christians were winning anything. A mere 64 years after Jesus' birth, a fire burned Rome to the ground. Emperor Nero blamed the fire on Christians—something that led to widespread persecution of them.

With the exception of John, all of Jesus' closest friends—including Matthew—were killed because of their faith in him. Even though John wasn't martyred for his faith, he was forced to live in exile on an island. There was no happily ever after for him either.

The authors of the Gospels wrote about Jesus not from the position of victors but from the position of losers. As losers, there was no reason for them to engage in propaganda, because there was nothing for them to protect—not even their lives.

Instead, having experienced the Good News of Jesus for themselves, they couldn't help but write it down so others could experience it. They wrote about all they'd seen and heard in regard to a sinless God/man named Jesus, even though they knew that doing so might cost them their lives. They told the good, the bad, and the confusing and in so doing, portrayed Jesus as a complex person with rich emotions.

That's not what victors trying to cover up something do.

It's not what winners trying to spread a uniform version of the truth do.

It's what people who have nothing to hide do.

JESUS Talk

1. In this chapter, Jen offers several reasons why she doesn't believe Jesus committed sins (which, so the theory goes, might have been left out of the Bible). Which reasons do you find most compelling? Why?
2. The Gospels weren't written by the winners. They were written by the losers. In what ways were Christians "losing" at the time the Gospels were written?
3. Why's it important that the Gospels were written by people who were losing and not winning?
4. In light of this chapter, do you think Jesus' sins were simply left out of the Bible? Why or why not?

Section Seven
Why Did JESUS Die?

"God sent Jesus to take away all our sins so we can live for eternity with him when we die, which is cool."

— NIKKO

33: What Does It Mean that JESUS Died for Us?

December 13.

It's the date—decades apart—when my grandma was born, married, and buried. She died my freshman year of high school, roughly five months after being diagnosed with cancer. For four of those months, she lived with us. During that time, I saw her lose most of her hair from one lone round of chemotherapy. I watched as she got weaker and weaker, eventually even having to wear adult diapers.

Though I wasn't actually home, I vividly remember the day Grandma died. That afternoon, I'd flown to St. Louis to spend the weekend with my aunt. Shortly after landing, I called home to let my parents know I'd arrived safely.

My mom was tense when she answered the phone. When I asked what was wrong, at first she tried to avoid the question. I pushed and she eventually screamed, "I think she's dying!"

I don't remember much after that other than Mom finally calling us back to let us know that Grandma had died. That's when we learned how it happened. Mom had gone grocery shopping and returned home to find my Grandma lying on the kitchen floor in my dad's arms. Apparently she'd gotten up to use the bathroom and then collapsed. She died, cradled in my dad's arms.

My aunt and I flew home the next day. Two days later, we held Grandma's wake. During it, a number of people told me, "She lived a good, long life." And she did—she was nearly 81 years old. But somehow that wasn't comforting, especially when, on the next day, instead of celebrating Grandma's birthday, we watched as her coffin was closed for the last time.

As a 14-year-old, there was very little I understood about death.

What I knew, beyond a shadow of a doubt, was that death was ugly and hard.

Even though our faith in Jesus gives us the assurance of eternal life, it's not easy to watch those we love suffer and die. Since we don't know exactly what to expect after death, death is scary—especially since we know we will one day face it. We don't know how or when death will come, but we know it will. It's part of the human experience, which means that if Jesus was fully human he, too, had to die.

Unlike my grandma, though, Jesus didn't live a good long life. Around the age of 33, he died a horrific death by crucifixion—the most humiliating and gruesome method of execution there was at the time. It was so grotesque that Romans reserved it for only the worst criminals.

Those sentenced to crucifixion were stripped and then nailed to a cross in a public place for all to see. Unlike more modern methods of execution, those who were crucified didn't die quickly. Instead, they suffered for hours.

You see, in order to breathe while nailed to a cross you have to push up on your feet. The only problem is your feet are nailed to the cross, along with your hands, which are spread far apart. As a result, breathing takes enormous effort and causes extraordinary pain. Eventually, your body wears out and you can't push up any more so you slowly suffocate.

Interestingly, none of these gory details are found in the Gospels—the four books that tell us about Jesus' life, death, and resurrection. Instead, the writers of the Gospels focus their attention elsewhere.

Take, for example, Mark's account of Jesus' crucifixion. Rather than tell us exactly how many breaths Jesus took on the cross, or how horrific the scene was, Mark tells us that "at the sixth hour darkness came over the whole land until the ninth hour" (Mark 15:33).

The sixth hour is actually noon, which means that on the day Jesus died, it was completely dark during the time when the sun is typically the brightest. This means that this darkness was supernatural—it was a sign of God the Father's judgment, not altogether different from the plague of darkness God the Father sent to try to convince the Egyptian Pharaoh to free his chosen people. The question is, who's God the Father judging?

It's easy to assume God the Father is judging the people crucifying Jesus. Or maybe even to assume that he's judging us since our sins put Jesus on the cross. After all, that's what it means that Jesus died *for us,* right?

But what if, at the crucifixion, God the Father is actually judging his only son, Jesus?

> "Jesus died to prove himself, to prove God, to prove heaven, and to send hope to his people."
> — JESSICA

After all, if Jesus died *for us,* that means he got what *we* deserved—not just our punishment, but our judgment as well.

If that's the case, then no wonder Jesus cries out, "My God, my God, why have you forsaken me?" (Mark 15:34).

To be forsaken means to be totally and completely abandoned. And on the cross, Jesus was.

Notice that he doesn't cry out, "God! Why have you forsaken me?" He cries out "*My* God."

My shows possession. It shows intimacy.

When I talk about my parents I say *my* mom or *my* dad. The same is true of *my* husband and *my* daughter. Doing so conveys a sense of belonging: I belong to them and they belong to me.

The same is true of God the Father and Jesus. Jesus cries out "*my* God" because as God's only Son, he belongs to God the Father. Even though he's fully human, he's never been apart from God. He's never NOT known God's love. In his own words, "I and the Father are one" (John 10:30).

Maybe, then, the answer to Jesus' question, "Why have you forsaken me?" isn't rhetorical. In the words of pastor and author Timothy Keller, maybe the answer to Jesus' question is actually, "For you, for me, for us. Jesus was forsaken by God so that we would never have to be. The judgment that should have fallen on us fell instead on Jesus."[3]

With that in mind, when we say "Jesus died for us," we're not saying Jesus died so we won't have to. Like it or not, Christian or not, like my grandma, you and I will still die someday. What we won't do is experience complete and utter abandonment by God the Father.

To give us proof of this, Mark includes this detail in his account of Jesus' death: "The curtain of the temple was torn in two from top to bottom" (Mark 15:38).

It's tempting for you and me to read this and think: "So what?"

---

3. Timothy Keller, *Jesus the King* (Riverhead, 2011), 221.

In reality, the tearing of the temple curtain is a HUGE deal. You see, in Jesus' time, the temple curtain was heavy. It more closely resembled a wall than the drapes hanging in your living room.

This curtain was used to separate the holy of holies—which is the part of the temple where Jews believed God's presence dwelled—from the rest of the temple. Only the holiest priest could enter this space once a year, on the holiest day of the year, Yom Kippur, in order to offer a sacrifice for people's sins. Commoners like you and I would never have been allowed in this part of the temple, in the very presence of God.

So when this curtain rips—at the exact moment Jesus died, it's like God the Father is literally tearing it up and saying, "You won't be needing that anymore. Because of Jesus' death, YOU can now come into my presence."

> "Jesus died to save us and because he wasn't going to fight back when he was sentenced to death."
>
> — TAYLOR

That's what it means to me that Jesus died for us: Jesus got what we deserved so that we can get what he deserved: life with God—now and forever.

Now that you know what it means to me, what does it mean to *you* that Jesus died for us?

That's the question we'll be exploring in this section. To do so, we'll look at four different atonement theories—the substitutionary atonement theory, the ransom theory of atonement, the representative theory of atonement, and the theology of the cross. These theories are called *atonement* theories because to atone for something means "to make right," "to make amends," or "to offer a payment for a wrongdoing." In essence, that's what Jesus' death on the cross did: It made us right with God.

Each of the atonement theories we'll be looking at answers our question, "What does it mean that Jesus died for us?" a little differently. Even so, each of them is still rooted in Scripture. Each is centuries old.

Some of the atonement theories might be more familiar to you than others. Some might also make more sense to you. That's okay.

My prayer is that by learning how others answer the question, "What does it mean that Jesus died for us?" you'll be able to do the same.

JESUS Talk

1. Describe your first experience with death. Who died? What was that experience like for you?
2. Why do you think the Gospel writers left out most of the gory details surrounding Jesus' death?
3. At Jesus' death, who do you think God the Father was judging? Why?
4. What do you think it means that "Jesus got what we deserved so that we can get what he deserved"?
5. Prior to reading this chapter, how would you have answered the question, "What does it mean that Jesus died for us?" How would you answer that question now? Why?
6. Why does your answer to the question, "What does it mean that Jesus died for us?" matter?

"After we chose sin and walked away from the Lord, God's plan was centered on Jesus. He lived the perfect life to pay the debt for our sins. The just punishment [for our sins] is death. Jesus absorbed all of God's wrath for us. He saved us and through his resurrection we are given new life. We're given mercy by not being given the hell we deserve. We're given grace."

— ALEX

34: An Unblemished Sheep

As a general rule, I don't care for postapocalyptic stories. One exception to this is *The Hunger Games*. I enjoyed both the books and the movies.

As you may know, *The Hunger Games* is set in the country of Panem, which is divided into 12 districts. Decades earlier, these districts rebelled against the Capitol. As punishment, the Capitol instituted the yearly Hunger Games. During these games, each of the 12 districts is required to offer one boy and one girl as tributes. Tributes then fight one another to the death.

Early on in *The Hunger Games*, each district assembles for the day of reckoning, the day in which the districts' tributes are chosen. When Primrose Everdeen is chosen as District 12's tribute, immediately her sister, Katniss—the story's heroine—volunteers in her place. Like Primrose, she meets the requirements of a tribute. As a result, she's able to offer herself as a substitute for Primrose.

In a lot of ways, what happens in *The Hunger Games* is not unlike what happens through Jesus' death. Scholars call this way of thinking about Jesus' death *substitutionary atonement*.

According to the substitutionary atonement theory, like the districts in *The Hunger Games*, we, too, rebelled against the Capitol: God. This started in the Garden of Eden when Adam and Eve first sinned by disobeying God the Father and eating the fruit from the tree of knowledge of good and evil (Genesis 3). It's continued ever since, with all the ways we sin.

Since God the Father is perfectly holy, he cannot be around sin. Since we are sinners, our sin separates us from God, who's also perfectly just. Because he's just, he can't just let our sins slide. Letting our sins slide wouldn't be fair; it would be decidedly unjust. As a result, someone or something's got to pay for our sins.

Like the Capitol, God requires blood to be shed as punishment for our disobedience. According to Hebrews 9:22, "Without the shedding of blood, there is no forgiveness."

> "Jesus took our faults and made them his own and then died for us. He took everything we did wrong and like an innocent life was shed. That equates to all of our sins being saved."
>
> — BRIGID

Initially, people in biblical times paid their debts by sacrificing a perfect, unblemished sheep. But eventually, God the Father decided there needed to be a better sacrifice—a sacrifice that would pay our debt once and for all and eliminate the need for future sacrifices.

Now, for a sacrifice to pay our debt once and for all, that sacrifice had to be human. After all, since it's humans who disobeyed God the Father, it's humans—not sheep—who have to be punished. For something to be an acceptable sacrifice, it also has to be perfect and unblemished. In other words, it's got to be sinless. That's problematic because as we know, all humans are sinful.

God the Father had to figure out another way. So he sent his one and only Son, Jesus, to earth—fully human. As we've learned, during his time on earth, Jesus experienced everything we do. The one difference is he never sinned. He remained perfect.

Because he did, he fulfilled the requirements needed to be a sacrifice. So just as Katniss willingly substituted herself for Primrose, Jesus willingly substituted himself for us.

He got the punishment we deserved because of our sins: a brutal awful death on the cross. That's why his cousin, John the Baptist, called Jesus the "Lamb of God, who takes away the sin of the world" (John 1:29).

> "Jesus was the ultimate sacrifice. Before, people gave a lamb for their sins. But Jesus was for everyone."
>
> — MADELEINE

Thanks to Jesus, our punishment has been paid. The shedding of his blood satisfied God's justice once and for all.

And that's where Jesus' death differs from the Hunger Games. Unlike the Capitol, God is also loving and merciful. So now that the perfect sacrifice has been offered, he doesn't require any others. Through Jesus' death on the cross, our debt has been paid and we are forgiven, now and always.

JESUS Talk

1. According to the substitutionary atonement theory, why did Jesus die?
2. How does the substitutionary atonement theory account for a loving God? A just God?
3. Read Hebrews 9:22. Why is blood required for forgiveness? According to the substitutionary atonement theory, how does Jesus' death on the cross result in our forgiveness?
4. Read John 1:29. What does it mean that Jesus is the Lamb of God?
5. Like all theories, there are problems with the substitutionary atonement theory. Like what?
6. Prior to reading this chapter, how familiar were you with the substitutionary atonement theory? In what ways has this atonement theory shaped your own answer to the question, "Why did Jesus die?"

> *"Satan is like the kidnapper, luring humanity in with the tree of knowledge (similar to candy). But God paid our ransom through Jesus' death, so that the kidnapper would not keep us."*
>
> — BECCA

35: Ransomed

As a young child, I remember learning about "stranger danger" in school. Stranger danger taught me never to take candy from a stranger and to stay away from big white creeper vans. It also encouraged my family to establish a secret password. The idea behind that was this: If my parents ever needed to send a stranger to pick me up from someplace, I was to ask that person for my family's password. If that person knew it, my parents had really sent her. If not, she was a dangerous stranger trying to kidnap me. If that was the case, I was to scream loudly and run as fast I could to escape this threat.

Combine this with reading crime novels as well as watching the news, movies, and hundreds of episodes of *Law and Order* and for a while, I was convinced that most people were kidnapped at some point in their lives and either killed or held for ransom—a large chunk of money used to buy your freedom. Thanks to the influence of *Law and Order,* I also knew that ransoms were typically so large that those who had to pay them had to sacrifice something in order to do so. Since I knew my parents had only a modest income, I worried how they would ever be able to scrape together the ransom my kidnappers would inevitably demand from them.

Of course, much to my relief, I was never actually kidnapped so no one ever had to pay a ransom for me...

Unless, that is, you count Jesus.

You could argue that Jesus bought my—and your—freedom with a ransom. Only the ransom he paid for us wasn't money. It was his death on the cross.

According to this way of thinking about Jesus' death—something scholars call the *ransom theory of atonement*—when Adam and Eve ate the fruit from the tree of the knowledge of good and evil in the Garden of Eden, they bargained away humankind's freedom for all eternity. They sold our souls to Satan, who kidnapped our eternal life. So without intervention, our fate would be far worse than that of a kidnapping victim on *Law and Order:* It'd be an eternity in hell.

Thankfully, God the Father offered his son, Jesus, as a ransom to Satan for us. Jesus himself describes this exchange in Mark 10:45 when he says, "For even the Son of Man did not come to be served, but to serve and to give his life as a ransom for many."

By saying that he didn't come to be served, Jesus is saying that, like every other king throughout history, he has every right to expect people—including us—to serve him. Rather than demand we do, he does something radically different. He serves us by giving his life as a ransom to Satan for our souls.

> "Jesus payed the ultimate price—or ransom—so that we would not have to go to hell. He kind of payed off the devil."
> — ELLE

The price of the ransom Jesus paid for our souls is the highest anyone could ever demand: his own life. According to Jesus' friend and apostle John in the book of Revelation, with Jesus' blood, he "purchased" us for God (Revelation 5:9).

Since Jesus paid the ultimate price for our freedom from Satan, we can be confident that we are extraordinarily valuable. We matter deeply to God, who now calls us to serve him and others. We can do so freely because we know that Satan—the greatest threat to our existence, a threat far greater than any "stranger danger" could ever be—has already been eliminated by Jesus' death on the cross.

JESUS Talk

1. According to the ransom theory of atonement, why did Jesus die?
2. How does the ransom theory of atonement account for a loving God? A just God?
3. According to Jen, "Since Jesus paid the ultimate price for our freedom from Satan, we can be confident that we are extraordinarily valuable." Do you really believe this? Why or why not?
4. Like all theories, there are problems with the ransom theory of atonement. Like what?
5. Prior to reading this chapter, how familiar were you with the ransom theory of atonement? In what ways has this atonement theory shaped your own answer to the question, "Why did Jesus die?"
6. How does the ransom theory of atonement compare to the substitutionary theory of atonement? Which makes more sense to you? Why?

"God the Father can't just go out and show up on earth. Everyone would be like, 'You're new. We don't know you. We've never seen anything like this.' Instead, God brought a man into the world. Jesus grew up like any other kid. He made friendships. There was more a connection with society and Jesus. God used Jesus to make believers."

— KATHERINE

36: Represent

I spent five years working in a mostly Korean congregation.

Here's the thing: I'm a white female.

For those five years, I was in the minority. And while I learned a ton during this time, it was also incredibly hard.

If you've ever been in the minority, you know what I mean.

It's hard being the odd man or in my case, woman, out.

It's hard not understanding stuff like language, inside jokes, or even foods. I'm a picky eater, so I still remember how overwhelmed I was when I attended my first function at my mostly Korean congregation, desperately searching for food I could recognize among bulgogi, kai bi, and kim chi. On my first mission trip, one of my teens opened a package of spicy squid and the smell made me want to hurl. When they offered me a piece, I wanted to cry, because it was so foreign to me. All I wanted was familiar comfort food like a nice box of Cheez-Its.

It's also hard navigating cross-cultural relationships. My husband and I once attended the wake of a student's grandma. We showed up about an hour after the wake began, thinking we'd pay our respects and leave, like we were accustomed to doing. Imagine how embarrassed we were when we walked in to what we quickly realized was the middle of a worship service. As it turns out, different cultures do wakes very differently from one another.

To make sense of these situations, I quickly learned I needed a representative who understood both the American and Asian culture to explain and interpret things for me. Thankfully, I had such a person.

One of my friends and adult leaders, Jean, was Korean-American. Jean was born in Korea but came to the United States when she was very young. She was raised by Korean-speaking parents who immersed her in the Korean culture. Because of this, she speaks Korean fluently and understands it well. Jean also grew up going to American schools and surrounded by American culture. As a result, she understands it too.

When I needed someone to translate because of a language barrier, Jean willingly did so, making it possible for me to communicate with people I would otherwise not have been able to understand. When I had to navigate a Korean food line, Jean would go in front of me, explaining what each item was and suggesting foods I might enjoy. She'd also explain traditions—like Korean wakes—to me so that I could better understand and appreciate the Korean culture.

The beauty of having Jean serve in this role was that in addition to representing the Korean culture to me, she could also represent me to our first-generation Korean parents—those for whom the American culture was still very foreign. She could explain why in addition to worshiping, we also played games and spent time talking with each other at every youth ministry gathering we held.

Jean could serve in this representative role because she wasn't just Korean *or* American but Korean-American.

Just as I needed a representative to help me navigate cross-cultural relationships at my mostly Korean congregation, in order to relate to God the Father we also need a representative. Since God the Father is otherworldly, try as he might, he cannot actually relate to us. He's never walked in our shoes. Similarly, since we aren't perfectly holy, we cannot fully relate to him. Our experiences are too different; the gap between us too wide. In order to relate to one another, someone has to bridge the gap between us.

> "Jesus fully understands human life, yet he also fully understands God because he's both. Therefore, it makes him relatable and knowledgeable about God."
>
> — ANDREW

Thankfully, since as we learned in Section 2, Jesus is not just God or human but a God/man, he's uniquely qualified to bridge the gap; to be our representative to and for God the Father. Scholars call this way of thinking about Jesus' death the representative view of atonement. It's the third atonement theory we'll explore in this section.

According to the representative view of atonement, since Jesus was fully human, he understands people in a way that God the Father does not. That makes him uniquely qualified to talk to God the Father on our behalf and do so in a way that, because he's also God, makes sense to God the Father. That's what Paul means when he tells Timothy, "For there is one God and one mediator between God and men, the mankind Christ Jesus" (1 Timothy 2:5).

As our mediator, Jesus is the go-between for us and God the Father. He pleads our case to God the Father because he's fluent in both the language of God and humans. He's fluent in the ways of God and humans—he knows how we think and operate. He also knows how God the Father thinks and operates. That's why he's qualified to not only be our representative to God the Father, but to be God the Father's representative to us.

Just think about how often you've heard people question,

> *"Where is God?"*
> *"How can God allow evil to happen?"*
> *"Why do bad things happen to good people?"*

Maybe you've even asked these questions yourself. I know I have.

Whenever we do, we're essentially asking God to show himself, even in and among the bad things that happen in our world.

That's exactly what Jesus does on the cross and throughout his entire life.

"Jesus is the Son of God. He's the bridge between us and God."

— TINA

He heals the sick, feeds the hungry, forgives the sinners, hangs out with the outcasts, and brings hope to a weary world. All the while, he represents God the Father to us; he shows us God the Father.

Jesus does what my friend Jean did for me when I worked at the mostly Korean church: He interprets and bridges cultural gaps we wouldn't otherwise understand. This, in turn, makes it possible for us to communicate, understand each other, and ultimately enter into a relationship with one another.

the real **JESUS**

JESUS Talk

1. Describe a time when you needed a representative.
2. How has Jesus shown you God the Father?
3. According to the representative theory of atonement, why did Jesus die?
4. How does the representative theory of atonement account for a loving God? A just God?
5. Like all theories, there are problems with the representative theory of atonement. Like what?
6. Prior to reading this chapter, how familiar were you with the representative theory of atonement? In what ways has this atonement theory shaped your own answer to the question, "Why did Jesus die?"
7. How does the representative theory of atonement compare to the substitutionary and ransom theories of atonement? Which makes the most sense to you? Why?

"Maybe it's okay to simply accept that life sucks but that Jesus has felt our pain so we can rest in the hope that he is always with us; that God will continue to deliver us from our heartbreak; and in the anticipation of being used to help make the world a little less broken."

— EMILY

37: Life Is Hard but God Is There

I'll admit, I've lived something of a charmed life.

I'm an only child, which some might argue makes me inherently spoiled. I graduated high school as the valedictorian of my class. I applied to one college and got in. It was also my top choice of schools. I fell in love and married my college sweetheart just a few months after graduation. My husband and I both graduated college with no debt. We both landed jobs immediately after college graduation. Within two years of being married, we bought a house.

This isn't to say our life has been perfect... It hasn't been. We've lost jobs, moved, and had people close to us die. But for the most part, our life has been good.

Until that, is, two years ago, when we experienced a new kind of suffering. I had a miscarriage; our baby died inside me. It was a horrible time in our life together—the worst kind of suffering we'd ever known or experienced. It also coincided with Holy Week—the week in the church year we spend remembering the death of Jesus.

In my congregation, Holy Week is a BIG deal. On Sunday, we celebrate Palm Sunday, the day Jesus rode triumphantly into Jerusalem to cries of "Hosanna." On Monday through Wednesday, we worship nightly. Each night explores a different part of Jesus' final week, including the night on which Jesus was betrayed by one of his best friends, Judas.

Thursday is the start of what we call "The Great Three Days." On Thursday, we read the story of Jesus' last supper with his apostles. Then we wash each other's feet. On Friday, we read the story of Jesus' arrest, trial, and crucifixion and have the chance to pray in front of a giant cross in order to remember what Jesus did for us on the cross. On Saturday, we tell the story of our faith—from creation to the prophets, emphasizing how each part of the story points to Jesus.

In the past, I've never really enjoyed Holy Week. It always felt to me like we spent a whole lot of time dwelling on Jesus' death.

I'd much rather skip that and get to the good stuff: Easter and the story of Jesus' resurrection.

The year I miscarried, I felt differently. That year, I experienced the cross in a new way.

Prior to that week, I'd always associated the incarnation—that's the fancy word we use to describe how God became like us—with Jesus' birth. And certainly, as we've seen, Jesus' birth is definitely a moment in which Jesus was very much like us.

That year, though, the place where I most saw Jesus' humanity was at his death, specifically in the moment when he cried out in anguish from the cross, "My God, my God, why have you forsaken me?"

The week I lost my baby, I cried similar words. I cursed God. I questioned, "Why?" and "Where are you God?"

I got no audible answers. But in worship that week, as we remembered the story of Jesus' suffering and death, I was comforted. I felt his presence with me.

Prior to that, I'd always answered the question "Why did Jesus die?" by saying, "To save us from our sins."

As we've seen, that's true.

But that year, I learned there's more to the answer than that.

Jesus died so God could intimately know the pain that's part of our human experience.

That week, in the midst of terrible grief, when God the Father felt unapproachable to me, Jesus didn't. That week, the cross gave me permission to mourn—to cry, scream, and wail against God and the injustices of this world. It allowed me to see God not just as some distant, all-powerful being but as someone who's there with us in the midst of our suffering.

What I learned that Holy Week was what the great theologian Martin Luther talks about in something we call his theology of the cross: God is found, not in power but in weakness and suffering. The theology of the cross is the fourth and final atonement theory we'll explore in this section.

"Being a Christian doesn't exempt us from pain. God never promised that being a Christian would be easy. What He did promise is that it would be worth it."

— BRADLEY

According to the theology of the cross, there will always be times when life is hard. But because of Jesus' death on the cross, we can know beyond a shadow of a doubt that when we suffer, we are not alone. God is there.

In response to the question "Why do bad things happen to good people?" the theology of the cross answers not with empty words but with a person: Jesus.

The theology of the cross says that as much as the cross is about paying a penalty, it's also about redemption. As much as it's about death, it's also about life.

No matter how charmed your life seems right now, eventually something will go wrong. When it does, you'll likely question like I did, "Where are you God?"

The theology of the cross points directly to Jesus on the cross and says we may not like it, we may not be able to explain it, but that's where God is: there on the cross.

JESUS Talk

1. Describe the worst day of your life. What happened? According to the theology of the cross, where was God on that day?
2. How is the cross about redemption and life?
3. According to the theology of the cross, why did Jesus die?
4. How does the theology of the cross account for a loving God? A just God?
5. Like all theories, there are problems with the theology of the cross. Like what?
6. Prior to reading this chapter, how familiar were you with the theology of the cross? In what ways has this atonement theory shaped your own answer to the question, "Why did Jesus die?"
7. How does the theology of the cross compare to the substitutionary, ransom, and representative theories of atonement? Which makes the most sense to you? Why?
8. In this section, we've looked at several answers to the question "Why did Jesus die?" How does your congregation answer that question?
9. After reading this section, how would you answer the question, "Why did Jesus die?"

Section Eight
The Difference JESUS Makes

"I don't think every single day, 'This is what Jesus did for me. Thank you so much.' But I try to follow the example he set. I've given myself moral standards. I've followed them. I hate cheating. In my Latin class, everyone does it. Now people know me as this girl who won't cheat. It's not so much, 'Oh, thank you, Lord' but this is how I should live because this is how he lived."

— CALLIE

38: What a Ride!

Several of my high school friends' dads were police officers.

This didn't matter much to us until we started driving.

As we became more and more comfortable driving, we'd inch our way over the speed limit. Occasionally, we'd get pulled over. When we did, my friends with police officer dads NEVER got a ticket. They'd casually mention their dad's name along with what precinct he worked in, and bam... like magic, we'd be on our way. When it came to traffic violations, my friends had something of a "get out of jail free" card they could use whenever they screwed up.

In the same way, sometimes we treat Jesus as a "get out of hell free" card. When we do, we view Jesus' death and resurrection as something that might matter later—after we die—but that has little or no impact on our life now.

Sure, we occasionally touch base with Jesus through prayer or by attending church. Usually, though, our motivation for doing so is guilt. We fear that if we don't check in, our get out of hell free card might expire the moment we need it most.

In reality, though, Jesus is much more than a get out of hell free card. In John 10:10, Jesus tells his disciples, "The thief comes only to steal and kill and destroy; I have come that they may have life and have it to the full."

Sometimes, I think those of us who are Christians mistakenly confuse Jesus for the thief who comes to steal and kill and destroy rather than the one in whom we have life. We think that Jesus came to steal our freedom, to kill our fun, and destroy our relationships. In reality, though, Jesus came so that we might have life and have it to the full. Nowhere in Scripture does it say the full life that Jesus came to give us begins *after* we die.

"Jesus showed us the right way of life. He showed us all the good things we could do. He saved us from going with the crowd."

— SARAH

In fact, Scripture makes the opposite point. Time and time again, through his relationships with people, miracles, forgiveness of sins, and even his teachings, Jesus brings life to all whom he encounters.

Even now, Jesus' life, death, and resurrection continue to bring us life. Here's what I think the full life Jesus gives us might look like:

A full life is a beautiful thing. It's one lived surrounded by family and friends—some who follow Jesus and some who do not. It's one where you work hard and play hard, but you follow Jesus in all aspects of your life. It's also one in which you rest because you know there's one Savior and you're not him. A full life is one in which people matter more than things and since they do, you consistently give your money and yourself, knowing that doing so benefits both you and others. A full life is filled with adventure. It's a life in which you dare to take risks even though you know that you'll fail. It's one in which you're confident that when you mess up, you're forgiven. It's one where your identity and security comes not from anything you have or do, but from whose you are. It's one measured in love, where no matter how hard life gets, you still have hope.

Following Jesus is the adventure of a lifetime. It's something that makes our lives fuller and more meaningful. Far from being a get out of hell free card, it's something that makes a difference in our lives each and every day.

"Jesus taught us how to live, in every sense and every way."

— HOLLY

One of my heroes is a man by the name of Mike Yaconelli. Mike was a pastor, a lover of people, and an author. He was, in many ways, the embodiment of this verse and what it means to live life to the full. Shortly before his death, Mike said, "If I were to have a heart attack right at this moment, I hope I would have just enough air in my lungs and just enough strength in me to utter one last sentence as I fell to the floor: 'What a ride!' My life has been up and down, careening left then right, full of mistakes and bad decisions, and if I died right now, even though I would love to live longer, I could say from the depths of my soul, 'What a ride!' "

Like Mike, may we, at the end of our earthly lives, be able to say from the depths of our soul, "What a ride!" and know that we truly lived life to the full... Not in spite of Jesus, but because of him.

JESUS Talk

1. Have you ever thought about Jesus' death as a get out of hell free card? How did viewing Jesus' death as a get out of hell free card impact your faith?
2. John 10:10 says, "The thief comes only to steal and kill and destroy; I have come that they may have life and have it to the full." In what ways have you treated Jesus like a thief rather than the giver of life?
3. Why do you think so many people believe the full life Jesus came to give us begins only after we die?
4. To you, what does it mean that Jesus has given you life to the full?
5. If you were to die tomorrow, would you be able to say, "What a ride!" about your life? Why or why not?
6. Do you really believe that following Jesus is the adventure of a lifetime? Why or why not?

"Jesus is the one who made you into the person you are today."
— STEVE

39: I'm His

How do you define yourself?

Are you a jock? A musician? A drama geek? A band nerd? A brain?

Throughout high school, I was definitely a brain. I graduated as valedictorian—an accomplishment I worked hard for. Being the "smart girl" was my identity.

In some ways, that was good. I mean, I definitely wasn't athletic. Ever since I got hit in the mouth with a baseball, I'd preferred running AWAY from flying objects hurling towards me than running towards them in an effort to catch them.

I was also always super self-conscious about my appearance. I never felt pretty.

As a result, I found safety and security in excelling academically and knowing people thought I was smart. The problem is, I feared what would happen if, God forbid, my rank ever slipped to number two. By the time my senior year rolled around, as long as I did BETTER than the girl who was number two on a project or test, I didn't actually care about what my grade was, let alone whether or not I'd actually learned the material in question. In some ways, maintaining my class rank robbed me of the joy of learning. But alas, it allowed me to graduate as valedictorian.

It made my parents proud.

And again, it made me feel safe and secure... Until, that is, I got to my engineering classes at the University of Illinois.

Suddenly, I was in classes where EVERYONE had graduated as the valedictorian of their class; where there were people with higher ACT scores than mine; where I was no longer the smartest person in the room. For the first time in my life, I struggled to keep up with my classes. No matter how hard I studied, I couldn't quite grasp the material.

First semester freshmen year I got my first C in Chemistry 101.

For someone who had never even gotten a B during high school, this was devastating. Upon hearing the news, I literally cried for a week. I thought my world was ending. How could it not when this thing I had built my entire identity around was no longer true of me?

I wish I would have known then that our true identity comes from *whose* we are; not from anything we do or don't do.

I am a child of God created in God's image.

God came to earth in Jesus to show me I am loved.

I am valued.

I am worthy.

And so are you.

Don't believe me?

Consider this example from Jesus' friend John. In the Gospel of

John, there's a character who's consistently referred to as the "one whom Jesus loved" (John 13:23, NRSVA). Most people actually think this is how the writer of the Gospel—Jesus' friend and apostle John—referred to himself.

This used to drive me nuts. I'd read it and think, "What an arrogant man!" I mean, if Jesus loves everyone, how dare John think of himself as the "*one* whom Jesus loved"?

Then I realized I was really quite jealous of John. Like John, I wanted to believe that I too am the one Jesus loves. Don't you?

Far too often, I think Jesus only loves me when I'm perfect—which, by the way, is never... Or that Jesus only loves me when I'm doing great stuff for him.

Neither of those two things was true for John. He certainly wasn't perfect. He and the other apostles argued over which of them was the greatest. His mom even asked Jesus to give him a special position of power in his Kingdom. He also had a bit of a temper, wanting to rain down fire on an entire Samaritan village who refused to welcome Jesus.

Even so, John didn't get hung up on his failures.

Perhaps because he understood his primary identity had nothing to do with them... or with any of his successes. Instead, he recognized his primary identity came from his relationship with Jesus.

Ours does too.

As a child of God, you are loved, worthy, and valuable even when you...
  Fail a test
  Disappoint your parents
  Play a wrong note in your music recital

Forget your line during a show
Strike out
Miss a free throw
Let down your team
Betray your friend
Have a bad hair day
Get in a car accident
Get dumped by your significant other
Don't get the score you want on your ACT or SAT
Don't get into your top choice of college... or your second
    or third... or even your tenth
Can't get a job

As a child of God, you are loved, worthy, and valuable even when life turns out differently than you planned.

Your identity is not actually based on any of those things.

Instead, your identity comes from your relationship with Jesus.

Like John, YOU are the "one whom Jesus loves."

And because you are, you are chosen.

Worthy.

Accepted.

Valued.

Safe and secure.

Not just some of the time, but all of the time.

JESUS Talk

1. Answer the question that opens this chapter: How do you define yourself?
2. Your true identity comes, not from anything you do or don't do but from whose you are. How easy or difficult is it for you to believe this? Why?
3. Despite the fact that your true identity comes from whose you are, what have you done to try to earn Jesus' love?
4. How would your life change if you truly believed that you are the one whom Jesus loves?
5. As "the one whom Jesus loves," you are chosen, worthy, accepted, valued, safe and secure. Which of these words do you most need to remember? Why? How would doing so impact the way you see yourself?

"I think Jesus would hang out with the people you'd least expect. You'd think he'd be among the upper class. I think he'd be with people who are the lower class."

— KENT

40: The Outcasts

I went to a tiny grade school that encompassed grades K-8. For those nine years, I basically had the same kids in my class. Since it didn't happen very often, whenever someone moved away or a new student came, it was a big deal.

In 7th grade, a new girl I'll call Kim joined our class. To say Kim had a hard time fitting in is an understatement.

Not only was she new, but she had the misfortune of getting her period in the middle of a class shortly after she arrived. Since there was no way to hide the red stain on her white pants, everybody knew it. She was also overweight. And she had the worst acne of anyone in our class. She was teased relentlessly by the guys in our class who, one day, went so far as to ask her, "Would you rather be called *pig* or *earthquake?*"

I never made fun of Kim.

But I also never did anything to stop others from making fun of her, to stick up for or defend her, or even to sit with her in order to make her feel a little less alone.

Neither did anyone else.

Did I mention all of this took place at a Christian school?

And that as a part of our Christian school curriculum, my classmates and I took daily religious classes?

That's right.

Every morning, the pastor challenged us to follow Jesus. We frequently wrestled with the question "What would Jesus do?"

But it never occurred to me that my faith should impact how I treated Kim, perhaps because I didn't actually know what Jesus would do in this situation.

Maybe this is because in all my religion classes, we spent a lot more time speculating about what Jesus *might* do than looking at what Jesus actually did in Scripture.

Funny thing is, when you look at how Jesus treated people throughout his life, it quickly becomes obvious what he would have done in this particular situation. He would have befriended Kim, eaten lunch with her, and hung out with her—inside and outside of school.

How do I know this?

Because it's exactly what he did with Matthew, a tax collector.

Now, if you work, you might resent getting taxes taken out of your paycheck. Or maybe you've heard your parents complain about paying taxes. Despite our reluctance to give our government our hard-earned money, it's hard for us to comprehend how despised tax collectors actually were in Jesus' time.

In Jesus' time, the Jewish people—God's chosen people—lived under Roman occupation. As part of this, Rome collected taxes from the Jews. The people whose job it was to collect these taxes were called tax collectors. As we learned in **Chapter 17: Jesus Taught**, tax collectors were thought to be the scum of the earth because they made their money by stealing from others. Since they worked for the Romans, who were oppressing them, most Jews also considered tax collectors to be traitors.

Such is Matthew's lot in life. He's a tax collector, despised by people—except that is, by Jesus, who invites him to be one of his disciples, saying "Follow me." After doing so, Jesus goes to Matthew's house and eats dinner with him and a bunch of his tax collector friends, people known as sinners.

This gets a rise out of the Pharisees, who were the religious teachers of the time. In many ways, the Pharisees were the day's cool kids. They were respected, liked, and even idolized by others. Everyone wanted to be like them. When they see Jesus hanging out with the wrong crowd, they ask his disciples, "Why does your teacher eat with tax collectors and 'sinners'?"

"Jesus taught us how to break down walls."

— JUDY

In response, Jesus stays put, laughing and joking with his newfound friends, before turning to the Pharisees and saying, "It is not the healthy who need a doctor but the sick. But go and learn what this means, 'I desire mercy, not sacrifice.' For I have not come to call the righteous but sinners" (Matthew 9:9-13).

In other words, Jesus pretty much tells the popular kids, "These are my friends. I like hanging out with them and nothing you can say or do will make me stop. I'd like to hang out with you too, but to do that, you've got to be willing to come here and join *us*. These guys over here are my friends. So if you want to be my friend, you've got to be their friend too."

Throughout his ministry, Jesus has this conversation again and again with the popular crowd, who consistently question his choice to spend time with sinners like tax collectors, adulterers, and (*gasp*) women. Despite the opposition he continually faces for doing so, Jesus consistently chooses to hang out with the outcasts.

Had Jesus visited my grade school, I don't think he would have sat with me. He would have sat with Kim.

"Jesus taught us that everyone is accepted."

— HEIDI

As followers of Jesus, we'll do the same. We'll willingly befriend the Kims in our lives—the people others make fun of and reject. We'll do so no matter what it costs us, not because they're our projects but because they're our friends.

JESUS Talk

1. Which have you done more of: Speculate about what Jesus *might* do or look at what Jesus actually did in Scripture? Why do you think this is?
2. How might knowing how Jesus actually treated people in Scripture impact the way you treat others?
3. Think about the cafeteria at your school. With whom do you sit? With whom do you think Jesus would sit? Why?
4. Who's a "Kim" in your life? What might you risk by hanging out with your Kim? What might you gain? How would hanging out with the Kim in your life be following Jesus?

"I feel bad for the people who just go to church. If you're not going to fully expand your relationship with Jesus through community then why bother? Just sleep in."

— TIM

41: The Power of Touch

I love to travel. One of the most interesting places I've been is the island of Molokai in Hawaii.

When you think of Hawaii, you probably picture sun, gorgeous views, and the ocean. All of these things are true of Molokai. But what you may not know about this Hawaiian island is that it's also the home of a leper colony.

Leprosy might sound familiar to you. It's a horrific disease mentioned several times in Scripture. It involves the skin and nerves and was thought to be highly contagious. It causes the parts of the body that are infected to turn numb. As a result, those with leprosy are less likely to notice problems—like open sores—that can quickly become incredibly serious, sometimes resulting in disfigurement or the loss of limbs.

Prior to traveling to Molokai, I thought leprosy no longer existed.

As it turns out, even though there are now some treatments that help arrest leprosy, from Jesus' time through the 1800s when Kalaupapa, the leper colony on Molokai was formed, "treatment" was essentially the same: complete and utter isolation so as to protect other people from contracting the deadly disease.

It's the isolation that actually struck me most in Kalaupapa.

Kalaupapa is one of the most beautiful places on the planet. Its beauty is also what makes it such an ideal place for a leper colony. It's surrounded on three sides by the Pacific Ocean, so there's no easy way to get in and out of the colony. In fact, when the colony was first formed, the lepers, who arrived by ship, were told to jump overboard and swim for their lives. Once in the colony, there was no way for people to "escape." The only side of the colony not surrounded by the ocean was and is cut off from the rest of Molokai by 1600-foot sea cliffs that no one with leprosy could possibly climb. Those confined to this colony were once left completely and utterly alone—with few, if any, visitors and little to do except wait to die.

If this is how we treated those with leprosy 150 years ago when we knew a little bit about how diseases were transmitted, imagine how much worse life must have been for those in Jesus' time who had leprosy. They, too, were completely isolated from their family and friends, especially since according to Jewish law, their disease made them unclean. In every way, lepers were untouchable.

No wonder such people were desperate for healing. No wonder they were willing to go out of their way to see Jesus.

Luke tells the story of one such leper   a man who sees Jesus, falls to the ground, and begs him, "Lord, if you are willing, you can make me clean" (Luke 5:12).

In response, Jesus does something absolutely remarkable. He touches this man.

Since Luke doesn't give us many details about this man, we have no idea how long he'd been infected with leprosy. I tend to believe he's had it for quite some time. It's likely been months, if not years, since ANYONE has touched him.

But now, Jesus does just that. He compassionately touches a man who is untouchable.

In so doing, Jesus loves this man. He tangibly cares for him, giving him something no one else has been willing to give him for years: human contact.

Jesus also heals the man, saying, "Be clean!" (Luke 5:13).

Interestingly, the man's leprosy disappears NOT with Jesus' touch, but with his words. As a result, we know Jesus' touch wasn't necessary to heal this man of his leprosy. Yet, it was necessary to heal this man in other ways, to restore his value and dignity as a person.

In the same way, as followers of Jesus, you and I are called to be in community with others; to be close enough to physically touch others, just as Jesus did.

I learned the importance of touch when one of my good friends, Cindy, was diagnosed with lung cancer. For months, Cindy had been having noticeable difficulties breathing. My friends and I had all noticed that even walking up a single flight of steps often left her gasping for air. Yet, we never dreamed something serious was going on.

Now, as you might know, cancer is scary. Cindy's was especially scary because it was advanced when they caught it. In the days following her diagnosis, we felt helpless. So helpless and so scared that it was tempting to just disappear.

But we didn't.

Instead, we stepped closer in order to truly support Cindy and her husband, Greg. We muddled through awkward conversations and learned what to say. We also learned that sometimes the best thing we could do was simply sit with Cindy and Greg, saying nothing at all. We learned how to tangibly care for them by showing up at their house with dinner, or by dropping plants off in their backyard to give Cindy something beautiful to look at. We learned to go to the hospital whenever Cindy was stuck there and to actually reach out and hold her hand because touch really is powerful. We learned that in the midst of deep sorrow, you can still find things to laugh about.

When the worst happened and Cindy passed away, we learned to support Greg and be present—not just in the days immediately following Cindy's death, but in the months after that. We gave Greg permission to break down whenever he needed to and to rant and rave and cry out against the injustice of it all. We helped him figure out how to survive all the "firsts," like the first Thanksgiving and Christmas without Cindy. We also helped celebrate the small things, like Greg's decision to take a sabbatical and to get away from it all, with big parties.

To be sure, caring for Greg and Cindy during that time was emotionally difficult and physically draining. But our experience with them taught me that sometimes following Jesus leads us into other people's pain, where we risk feeling and experiencing pain *with* them. That's what compassion is.

"Jesus taught the importance of community and bringing people together."

— DENISE

Yet, when we're willing to actually experience people's pain, we become knit together in the most powerful kind of community there is: one that relies on Jesus for its strength and hope and one that is willing to follow Jesus' example to love and care for each other, tangibly and practically, even when life is hard. This kind of community is the most powerful kind of community there is, because through it, people's needs are met. People are healed—even when physical healing never occurs.

Whether you're 15 years old or 90, as a follower of Jesus, one of the differences he makes in your life is that he invites you to be part of this kind of community, a kind of community where no one is untouchable.

JESUS Talk

1. Even though his words were what healed the leper in Luke 5:12-13, Jesus chose to touch him. In doing so, what would Jesus have been risking?
2. In the story of the leper, Jesus touches the untouchable. Who at your school might be considered untouchable? How could you touch them? What might doing so mean to them? To you?
3. Describe a time when you have experienced the power of touch. Why do you think touch can be so powerful?
4. The most powerful kind of community there is one that relies on Jesus. Why? Are you a part of this type of community? If so, where? If not, why not? How could you go about finding such a community?

"I am surprised when I witness Christians who just simply believe. Just the other day in Bible study a girl next to me said, 'I feel like Jesus is telling me to spread this word with you.' What the heck? Jesus is talking to you? Are you sure that wasn't the person sneezing next to you? How do you know, without a single doubt, that Jesus is trying to communicate with you?"

— ABIGAIL

42: A Community of Doubters

If you could ask Jesus one question, what would it be and why?

Truthfully, it's hard for me to answer my own question—not because I don't have any questions for Jesus but because I have a bazillion questions for Jesus.

Questioning has always been an integral part of my faith. One of the things I loved about my high school youth ministry was that it was a place where I could always ask questions, where my friends and I could wrestle with our doubts and fears together in community. By not just allowing my questions but encouraging them, my youth group taught me that faith matters in real life.

When another one of the kids in our youth group was brutally attacked by a Rottweiler, leaving her with visible scars all over the upper half of her body, we wrestled with justice. Her parents demanded the dog be killed; she fought for it to be saved.

When my grandma was diagnosed with cancer, youth group was a place I could ask, "Where is God?"

When the dad of one the kids in our youth group had a very sudden brain aneurysm, not only was youth group a place for us to ask why, it was also a place for us to learn how to care for Charlie and his family.

As we got older and began dating, youth group was a place for us to learn about healthy relationships and wrestle with boundaries. It was also a place for us to wrestle with our vocations and what God might be calling us to do in college and beyond.

Because no question was off limits in my youth group, by the time I graduated from high school, I wholeheartedly believed no question was off limits to God.

"For me, believing isn't that easy. My faith is a daily struggle as I question all parts of Christianity."

— JEFF

Then I got to college. For the first time, I met people who believed doubting and questioning was wrong. In fact, I remember hearing again and again that there was no room for doubt in true faith. Often, the people telling me this would quote Jesus' words to his disciple Thomas, "Stop doubting and believe" (John 20:27).

It's easy to see why. At first glance, it seems like Jesus is telling Thomas, "Doubting is bad. Faith is good. Faith and doubt are opposites that can't coexist."

The more I've studied this passage, the less certain I've become that that's what Jesus's words actually mean.

In the days following Jesus' resurrection, Jesus makes several appearances to people, including his apostles. On one such occasion, he finds them huddled together behind locked doors, fearful that like Jesus they, too, will soon be arrested. All the apostles are there to see Jesus... except Thomas.

When Thomas shows up, his friends excitedly tell him, "We have seen the Lord!"

But Thomas refuses to believe them, saying, "Unless I see the nail marks in his hands and put my finger where the nails were and put my hand into his side, I will not believe it."

It's easy to judge Thomas for his comments.

Yet, had I missed Jesus' appearance to his apostles, I probably would have responded in the same way. Like him, I think I would have wanted to see Jesus for myself, to touch the scars from his crucifixion in order to see that he was real. Even today, I think faith would be much easier if we could see the proof Thomas demanded.

A week after Thomas makes his request, he and the other apostles are once again together, huddled behind locked doors. Suddenly, Jesus appears. When he does, he speaks directly to Thomas and says, "Put your finger here; see my hands. Reach out your hand and put it into my side. Stop doubting and believe" (John 20:24-27).

Notice the order here. Before Jesus tells Thomas to "stop doubting and believe," he grants Thomas his request. He invites him to touch his resurrected body so that he can have the proof he needs to believe. In doing so, Jesus meets Thomas in the middle of his doubts.

Knowing this, Jesus' command to stop doubting doesn't seem like a rebuke. Instead, it seems like someone saying, compassionately but maybe with a little bit of disappointment, "Now you've seen me with your own eyes. You've touched me. You have what you need so it's time to believe."

If that's what Jesus' words mean, we need not fear our doubts. Doubt can actually be a catalyst for faith. By honestly having the courage to wrestle with our questions and doubts, our faith can and will grow, pushing us closer to Jesus who, as he did with Thomas, will meet us in the middle of our doubts. Maybe belief is not the absence of doubts but the active pursuit of them.

Here's the catch though.

It's significant that Thomas' story happens in the context of community. Thomas admits his doubts to his friends, who are with him when Jesus shows up again to address him.

Likewise, we're not meant to wrestle with our doubts alone. Doing so can be dangerous, because it can be hard to find answers to our questions without help from anyone else. Instead of grappling with our questions alone, we're meant to face them with other people who can help us find answers and stay focused on Jesus, no matter how big our questions and doubts are. That's why my experience in my high school youth group was so significant for me.

"Every doubt I have allows me to dig deeper into my beliefs, building a strong foundation, so when I am truly shaken to the core, my faith will still be standing."

— MELISSA

So don't be ashamed or afraid of your questions and doubts. Instead, talk about them—with your parents, your youth group, and even your friends. When you do, you'll find Jesus there, waiting to meet you right smack dab in the middle of your doubts.

JESUS Talk

1. How would you answer the question at the start of this chapter: "If you could ask Jesus one question, what would it be and why?"
2. How do the people in your life typically react to doubt? Why do you think this is?
3. In light of this chapter, how do you interpret Jesus' words to Thomas in John 20:27, "Stop doubting and believe"?
4. Describe a time when wrestling with your doubts has actually caused your faith to grow.
5. Why do you think it's important to wrestle with our questions and doubts with others? How can you go about doing this if your community isn't open to doing so?
6. In the midst of your questions and doubts, when have you encountered Jesus?

"Jesus loved and cared about us and wanted to show that love and forgiveness are the best ways of solving conflict"

— PETER

43: Fight!

My favorite youth pastor, Kitty, left my congregation when I was a freshman in high school. Kitty was someone who everyone in our youth group loved. Not surprisingly, we took her loss hard.

From the beginning, the decks were stacked against her replacement, Noah. Although Noah was awkward, there wasn't actually anything wrong with him... except that he wasn't Kitty.

For that reason alone, we made Noah's life difficult.

Shortly after Noah began working with us, he scheduled a bike hike. Unlike Kitty, he never bothered to ask us whether or not that was something we'd like to do.

Rather than support him, I organized a boycott. The day of the bike hike, not one teen in our high school ministry showed up.

That afternoon, Noah called my house and left a message expressing his disappointment over the fact that no one showed up for the bike hike. Had it been up to me, I would have ignored his call. Unfortunately, back in those days, we had a household answering machine rather than individual cell phones. Upon hearing his message, my mom made me return the call.

When I did, Noah requested we sit down and talk our differences out, so that we could learn to work together. We scheduled a time to do so. Rather than go alone, I brought a couple adult leaders as well as a few other opinionated teens to the meeting, knowing they were on my side. I didn't bother to tell Noah I was planning on doing so.

What I remember most about our meeting is Noah's crestfallen face when I walked in with my entourage and his disappointment when he questioned why I felt the need to bring additional people to the meeting rather than just talk our conflict through with him.

In that moment, Noah was trying to show me a different, more healthy approach to conflict. He was living out the way Jesus calls us to deal with conflict—something Jesus shares in Matthew 18. According to Jesus, "If your brother sins against you, go and show him his fault, just between the two of you. If he listens to you, you have won your brother over" (Matthew 18:15).

Now, I realize *sin* is an awfully strong word here. Don't get distracted by it.

Whether or not I sinned against Noah isn't actually the point here. Clearly, we were embroiled in a conflict that needed to be resolved—for our sake as well as for the sake of our youth ministry. By inviting me to come talk to him, Noah did the hard thing, the Jesus-like thing. He was willing to face our conflict head on and deal with it, knowing that when conflict hits, ignoring it never helps a relationship—addressing it does.

Unfortunately, by coming to our agreed upon meeting with my army of supporters, I short-circuited this process. I didn't give Noah the chance to express his honest frustration with me; he never learned how much hurt and anger our group had over Kitty's departure. Because I short-circuited that process, we never really found a way to listen to, better understand, and forgive one another, which is Jesus' intent in the reconciliation process he outlines in Matthew 18.

According to Jesus, if the person who's screwed up won't listen to the one who's been hurt, then the next step in dealing with conflict is for the one who's been hurt to talk to that person again—this time with two or three other people.

To be clear, that's NOT what I was trying to do in our conflict with Noah. Had that been my intent, I would have brought *neutral* people to the meeting who might have helped Noah and I to hear one another. Instead, I brought people who were very clearly on my side. Doing so escalated our conflict rather than help resolve it.

Although this meeting happened early on in Noah's ministry at our church, for him, it was a breaking point. The message my actions sent him that day was that no matter how hard he tried, we weren't going to give him a chance. Not surprisingly, he left less than a year later.

When he did, we felt victorious. In our minds, we'd successfully gotten rid of the guy who was singlehandedly destroying our youth group.

In actuality, we're the ones who lost in that conflict. By the end of that year, our attendance had decreased, not increased. We'd also earned a reputation as a bratty, spoiled youth group capable of running people out. No one wants to work with that kind of group.

Had we been willing to courageously follow Jesus' model for dealing with conflict, there's not a doubt in my mind that our youth ministry would have better off—even if Noah remained in charge of it—than it actually was.

Maybe that's the whole point of Jesus' way of engaging with conflict.

It's hard, sure. It demands we have hard conversations with people, admit both how we've been hurt and how we've hurt others, confront our differences, and work through them—even when it's painful and difficult. But Jesus' way of dealing with conflict leads to reconciliation, to relationships that can continue to grow and maybe even flourish.

When it comes to conflict, I'd much rather walk away with intact relationships than a victory.

Wouldn't you?

JESUS Talk

1. How do you typically deal with conflict? How does this compare with how Jesus tells us to deal with conflict in Matthew 18:15-17?
2. According to Jen, "When conflict hits, ignoring it never helps a relationship." Do you agree or disagree? Why?
3. Why do you think it's so hard to deal with conflict in a healthy way?
4. How might your relationships benefit from following Jesus' approach to dealing with conflict?

"Even though school is my only real full-time job, and I don't have a boss making me come to work every day, it's my own expectations that keep me going non-stop from sun-up to way past sundown. Sundays, a day that is supposed to be reserved for rest and God, are my designated homework days on the weekends. After church I sometimes spend three to five hours holed up in my room, completing worksheets and studying for upcoming tests."

— SOPHIE

44: Nap Time

I love learning. Not surprisingly, I also loved school.

Back to school shopping was one of my favorite things ever—not shopping for clothes, mind you, but shopping for all of my school supplies.

I still remember the first time teachers required us to have an assignment notebook: a calendar in which we'd specifically write our assignments. It was the third grade, and I was quite sure these little calendars were straight from heaven. They appealed to every fiber of my being. They contained a calendar, perfect for the type-A kid I was. They also demanded organization (*yay!*) and gave me permission to make lists. To this day, I still create a daily to-do list and I still LOVE crossing things off it.

On days when I'm feeling overwhelmed, sometimes I'll intentionally include easy things on my list, like "take a shower," so that at the end of the day, I'll be able to cross at least one thing off my list. I know it's been a good day when at the end of it, most things are crossed off. But, I have a difficult time falling asleep if there are still lots of things on my to-do list.

When I go on vacation, my husband and I have an unplugging rule. We're not allowed to check email or any social media that might inadvertently remind us of work. This also means I've got to leave my calendar filled with to-do lists at home.

That's hard for me because resting is hard.

After all, I'm incredibly driven. I want to be successful. And I know that to be successful requires me to work hard, something I'm not afraid of.

Maybe you can relate.

Maybe you work hard, training and practicing so that you can excel at a sport and one day get a college scholarship to do what you love.

Maybe you practice music for several hours a day in order to perfect a piece for your upcoming concert.

Maybe you study for hours after school and even on the weekends, never allowing yourself to be satisfied with Bs when you know you can get As.

Maybe you work hard in your relationships, spending quality time with your best friend or significant other.

Maybe you spend hours at a job each week, diligently saving for a car or college or earning money to help your family make ends meet.

As Americans, we're taught to value a good work ethic. We've learned that if you work hard enough, anything is possible; your dream can and will come true. Phrases like "no rest for the weary" become our mantra.

To make matters worse, most of us suffer from a severe case of FOMO: fear of missing out. FOMO keeps our schedules full and our lives busy, so busy that even on weekends, we run from event to event.

Most of us don't like to rest.

Some of us don't even know how.

Enter Jesus.

Jesus knew how to sleep. He was such a master of sleeping that, as we've already seen, he was even able to sleep during hurricane-like storms. He was also someone who frequently retreated by himself in order to spend time with God the Father in prayer.

> "Being worn down by FOMO, school, social drama, and other responsibilities often leads to me leaving Jesus out of my daily life."
>
> — MARK

Sometimes, I'm baffled as to why the authors of Scripture include these seemingly inconsequential details in their accounts of Jesus' life. Wouldn't it have been better to include another miraculous healing or something profound that Jesus said? Why waste words saying Jesus slept or went off alone?

Then again, maybe in a culture as busy as ours, the thing we most need to hear is that Jesus rested.

And if we're supposed to follow Jesus' example, then shouldn't we rest too?

Absolutely. In fact, Jesus actually invites us to rest, saying, "Come to me, all you who are weary and burdened and I will give you rest" (Matthew 11:28).

Did you catch that?

Not only does Jesus invite us to rest, but he says that *he* we will give us rest.

True rest—the kind that allows you to lighten your load and share your worries—is found in the one who can actually do something about our worries.

One of the differences Jesus makes in our lives is that our belief in him allows us to confidently rest, especially since our value is not determined by how hard we work or how successful we become but by whose we are.

So go ahead.

Take a day off.

Sleep until noon. Then, rather than work—on school, music, sports, or your job—take a break. Don't run errands. Don't run from one event to the next. Instead, spend time with your family and friends. Go for a walk or ride your bike. Look at creation. Curl up with your cat and take a nap. Watch a movie. Spend time with God reading Scripture, journaling, or praying.

Do things that replenish you, that breathe life back into you, rather than add to your stress.

And do so even if your to-do list isn't finished. You can go back to completing it tomorrow.

As a follower of Jesus, you can rest without fear of missing out because you can trust that the place where you are is exactly the place God wants you.

As a follower of Jesus, you can rest because the world has one Savior and, try as you might, you're not it.

JESUS Talk

1. What's currently on your to-do list? Which of those things are life-giving? Which of those things are stressing you out?
2. Why do you think Scripture includes examples of Jesus resting?
3. Matthew 11:28 says, "Come to me, all you who are weary and burdened and I will give you rest." In what ways are you currently weary? How might Jesus give you rest?
4. What would your ideal day off look like? Why might it be difficult to take a genuine day off? How might doing so restore you?
5. According to Jen, "You can trust that the place where you are is exactly the place God wants you." Do you agree or disagree? Why?

"In order to become the best person you can be, it's necessary to accept and follow Jesus with your whole heart. You have to let his spirit and passion for justice and equality fill you and affect your actions."

— BETH

45: JESUS Staring Back at Me

I still remember the day my mom informed me that my high school youth ministry would be taking a mission trip to Tennessee rather than a canoe trip to the Boundary Waters.

I was MAD.

I had no interest in serving others—especially when doing so came at the expense of a trip I truly loved. So I asked my mom, "Why can't the poor people in Tennessee fix their own houses?"

She ignored my comment and instead informed me I was going. Her tone suggested I'd do well not to argue anymore.

The day we left for our summer mission trip, my friends and I were still ticked. Two days later, we pulled into our housing site—a school without air conditioning or showers—and immediately started complaining.

That night, a teen from each of our work crews had to go meet the family whose house we'd be working on. When no one else volunteered to go, our crew's adult leader informed me I'd be going. I reluctantly left my friends and drove with him an hour through the hollers of rural Tennessee to a small house in the middle of nowhere that was literally falling down. As soon as we got out of the car, chickens came running towards us, followed closely by a mangy dog. As we edged closer to the house, I couldn't help but notice the smell of the nearby outhouse. I thought to myself, "Oh great. This just gets better and better."

Eventually, we were ushered inside to meet the homeowner, an elderly woman with no teeth named Bert. She showed us around her house with the exception of her bedroom—where her dying husband, Chubs, was sound asleep. She then told us how excited she was that we were there to serve, how they'd been praying for an indoor bathroom that Chubs could get to more easily, and that we were the answer to their prayers.

That week, we worked hard to build Bert and Chubs a bathroom. We drywalled, installed plumbing, and laid linoleum. By the time we left, Bert and Chubs had the first indoor bathroom of their entire lives and, much to my surprise, my friends and I had a great week, largely because of the time we spent with Chubs.

Chubs was old and mostly bedridden. He had a long white beard and a potbelly that reminded us of Santa. He was extremely friendly—so much so that we began each day by visiting Chubs. Some days, he'd regale us with stories from his youth. Other days, he'd tell us about Bert, the love of his life. Still other days, we'd gather around his bedside and sing hymns like "Amazing Grace" and "How Great Thou Art." Always, Chubs would pray and then tell us about how lucky he was to be a follower of Jesus and how blessed he'd been his entire life because of that.

As a high school student, I was baffled by this. How could a dying man who literally had nothing— not even an indoor bathroom— call himself blessed just because he was a follower of Jesus?

"Jesus taught that everyone should serve others instead of expecting others to serve them."

— CARRIE

As I continued wrestling with this question, one of our group's adult leaders led a devotion for us on the parable of the sheep and the goats in Matthew 25:31-46. In this story, Jesus separates people into two groups, like a "shepherd separates the sheep from the goats."

He puts the sheep on his right-hand side and the goats on his left and then tells those on his right, "Come, you who are blessed by my Father, take your inheritance, the Kingdom prepared for you since the creation of the world. For I was hungry and you gave me something to eat, I was thirsty and you gave me something to drink, I was a stranger and you invited me in. I needed clothes and you clothed me. I was sick and you looked after me. I was in prison and you came to visit me" (Matthew 25:34-36).

Jesus' words confuse his followers—in much the same way that Chubs' words baffled me. Their confusion is evident in their response to Jesus. Essentially, they ask him, "When did we do all this stuff?" Jesus replies, "Whatever you did for one of the least of these brothers of mine, you did for me."

After reading this passage together, our leaders explained how that's what we were doing that week in Tennessee. By serving Bert and Chubs and the other homeowners, we were, in fact, serving Jesus.

In that moment, something started to click for me. I began to understand that following Jesus isn't just about knowing stuff; it's about doing stuff. It's about serving others.

"We are told to serve others and live with the poor, which stems back to Jesus' own childhood showing how human he is being born with truly nothing."

— RAY

And it isn't just about serving others during a week-long mission trip. It's also about serving others on a daily basis back at home— by feeding the hungry, giving drinks to the thirsty, welcoming the strangers, clothing the naked, taking care of the sick, and visiting those in prison.

By doing these things, we actually encounter Jesus. In the words of Mother Theresa, "Whenever I look into the eyes of a man dying from AIDS, I have the awareness that Jesus is staring back at me!"

As followers of Jesus, we don't serve because we have to. We serve others out of response to Jesus' abundant love for us. When we do, not only are the needs of others met, but we, too, are blessed as we see and encounter Jesus in new ways.

That was true for Mother Theresa. It was also true for me when I powerfully encountered Jesus in a dying man named Chubs.

May it be true for you as well.

JESUS Talk

1. What are your favorite ways to serve others?
2. By serving others, how are you serving Jesus?
3. Why is it important to serve others not just during week-long mission trips but also on a daily basis at home?
4. Think about your community. What needs do you see? How can you meet them?
5. In serving others, how have you encountered Jesus?

"Leadership is not about gaining power; it's about giving power."

46: JESUS-Style Leadership

Do you consider yourself to be a leader?

I didn't consider myself a leader until my sophomore English teacher called me one. I don't remember exactly how we came to be talking about leadership, but I distinctly remember my teacher saying, "Jen's a leader. When she talks, other people listen. People follow her."

That moment had a profound impact on me. Prior to that point, I always thought of myself as a shy girl—a trait that in my experience was not particularly conducive to leadership. All the leaders I knew were popular, extroverted, and very comfortable in front of other people. They weren't necessarily nice either, and I considered myself nice.

After my teacher publicly said this about me, however, I began to see myself in a new way. I began to think of myself as a leader and to pay attention to how others responded to what I said and did. I quickly took on more leadership positions in my high school youth ministry as well as in various clubs and groups at school.

As part of these leadership positions, I gradually acquired more authority. Being a leader in my high school youth ministry meant that I had the power to make decisions and even plan events. Being the newspaper editor meant that I had the power to assign articles, decide which we'd actually run, and even choose how visible they were in the paper. These decisions, in turn, had the power to influence what others in my high school were thinking and talking about.

Although I hate to admit it, I became a little addicted to the power that came with leadership.

It wasn't until I got to college that following Jesus began to impact my understanding of both leadership and power. One summer in college, I worked for an organization that runs week-long summer mission trips for high school students. On our last night of staff training, the speaker reflected on the story in the Bible where Jesus washes his disciples feet in an act designed to show his friends the full extent of his love (John 13:1).

This event occurs just before Jesus' betrayal and arrest. During it, Jesus gets up, takes off his outer clothing, and wraps a towel around his waist. He then goes to each of his disciples and washes their feet.

Now, to us, this story about feet and public washing seems a little weird. But in Jesus' time, people walked miles every day in flimsy sandals over sandy terrain. By the end of a day, their feet were filthy. It was, therefore, the custom for a servant to wash people's feet when they arrived at someone's house as a gesture of hospitality.

So when Jesus grabs a basin and a towel and washes his disciples feet, he's taking on the role of a humble servant—even though as he points out in John 13:13, he's rightfully their "teacher" and "Lord." To be clear, those who were teachers and lords would NEVER have lowered themselves to the position of a lowly servant stuck with the grossest job ever.

In so doing, Jesus models a new type of leadership—one that equates leadership not with power but with humble service. He then tells his disciples, including us, "I have set you an example that you should do as I have done for you. I tell you the truth, no servant is greater than his master, nor is a messenger greater than the one who sent him. Now that you know these things, you will be blessed if you do them" (John 13:13-17).

In other words, following Jesus means that when we lead, we do so as a servant.

> "Through his service, Jesus stepped down from his power and gave it to others. By doing these unprecedented deeds, like washing his disciples' feet, he both empowered others and gave us an example of true leadership."
>
> — MELANIE

At no time was this more evident to me than that night at my staff training when I participated in my first foot-washing service. That night, my boss's boss washed her feet and prayed over her. Then my boss washed my feet and prayed over me. Throughout the rest of the summer, we carried on this tradition, washing the feet of each of the adult leaders who came to serve. They then washed the feet of their students. Over and over again, we literally followed Jesus' example of servant leadership.

We did so in other ways too. That summer, my staff and I each led, but we did so as servants. When vans of high school students arrived each week, their adult leaders exhausted from hours (or sometimes days!) of driving, we met them outside and unloaded their vans for them, carrying piece after piece of luggage into our housing site. Throughout the week, we did the dirty jobs right alongside participants. We cleaned toilets, fixed meals, and washed dishes. After participants left at the end of the week, we cleaned the housing site in preparation for the next week's participants before then driving an hour away to shop for food for those participants. We did so week after week, despite our exhaustion, because to us, that's what following Jesus' example of servant leadership meant.

In the upside-down Kingdom of Jesus, the last will be first and the first will be last, power will be used for the good of others, and leaders will serve.

As it turns out, my sophomore self's understanding of leadership wasn't quite right. What makes a leader isn't a person's personality or popularity or whether they're introverted or extroverted. What makes a leader is a person's willingness to serve.

JESUS Talk

1. Answer the question at the start of this chapter, "Do you consider yourself to be a leader?" Why or why not?
2. Why do you think we tend to equate leadership with power?
3. What does servant-leadership look like to you?
4. According to Jen, "What makes a leader is a person's willingness to serve." Do you agree or disagree? Why?
5. What leadership positions do you hold? Who can you serve in those positions? How?

"I think a lot of people take Jesus for granted until things go rough like with financial problems. Then they wonder, 'Why would you do this to me?' Then life gets better. Things start to get better and they think, 'I did this by myself.' He's like, 'Hello! That's why I'm here.'"

— LILLY

47: There's Enough

Ever since I can remember, my parents taught me to save.

I remember going with my dad to open my first bank account. I was five. I also remember getting my allowance but being taught to save half of it each week. To this day, I get a little freaked out if my savings account gets low.

I mean, what happens if my husband and I were simultaneously laid off? Without adequate savings, how would we pay our bills? Or what would happen if we got sick and couldn't work any longer? Without savings, how would we survive?

"Jesus taught what is important and what is not. For example, love over money."

— SONJA

Like it or not, my desire to save also carries over into other less important aspects of my life. Take, for example, Cheez-Its, my favorite snack food ever. I love Cheez-Its so much that I hoard them. When I open a box, I'll hide it to prevent my husband from devouring them in a single sitting, lest we be left without Cheez-Its. (Never mind there's a grocery store five minutes from our house that carries an endless supply of Cheez-Its. When the zombie apocalypse hits, I'll be set.)

In order to make sure there's always enough, I save.

Here's the thing though. We don't worship a God who saves or hoards. We worship a generous God who gives extravagantly and makes sure there's always enough. Jesus' friend and apostle John makes this clear in his account of Jesus' first miracle.

In it, Jesus and his mom are at a wedding. While there, the host runs out of wine. To say this was a catastrophe is an understatement. It would have been like McDonald's running out of hamburgers—or in my case, the grocery store running out of Cheez-Its. In addition to creating problems for the guests (what would they drink without wine?), it would have also reflected incredibly poorly on the host.

Jesus' mom sees the problem and gently suggests Jesus might want to help their friend out. When Jesus refuses, she gets a little more insistent. Pretending not to hear his protests ("But, mom, I don't want to make wine!"), she tells the bus boys to do whatever Jesus says. So Jesus tells them to fill six water jugs with water, each containing 20-30 gallons of water (John 2:1-11).

In case math isn't your thing, that means that by the time they're done, Jesus has 120-180 gallons of water, which he promptly turns into wine. Now, even if we take the low end of that range, this means that Jesus produces approximately 3,028 servings of wine—far more than the host needs for his weddings guests. Jesus doesn't just give the wedding host *enough* wine to make do; he gives him an abundance of wine. In doing so, he shows us that he—God—is a generous God. In his Kingdom, there is always enough.

"Jesus will always provide. Sometimes what we need is not always physical, but he can provide for us spiritually."
— RICH

As followers of Jesus we, too, are called to be generous: to share our stuff and our money with others. No matter how much or how little of it we might have, we can do so without fear that we might one day be left with nothing because, you see, in the Kingdom of God, there's enough...

   ... love.

   ... money.

   ... and even Cheez-Its.

JESUS Talk

1. If "we worship a generous God who gives extravagantly and makes sure there's always enough" then how do you explain poverty?
2. When Jesus changes water into wine, he shows us that God is generous. How have you experienced God's generosity in your own life?
3. This week, how can you be generous with your time? Your stuff? Your money?
4. To you, what does it mean that in the Kingdom of God, there is always enough? Do you really believe this? Why or why not?

"I used to want to work with refugees. However, after a summer spent on the Pine Ridge Indian reservation, I want to work with Native Americans to help heal the pain in these places. There are many more populations that my heart aches for, but I can't save the whole world. God has already saved the whole world. God loved us all, so he gave us Jesus."

— DARBY

48: What Do You Want to Be When You Grow Up?

All I ever wanted to be was a teacher. But then one day in high school, my dad questioned my intent, saying, "Why would you want to do such a girly profession? A girl with your brains could do so much more."

That comment literally changed the course of my life. From that moment on, I set out to prove to my dad that I didn't have to settle for being a teacher. I chose instead to major in electrical engineering—a far less "girly" profession.

Almost from the beginning, I hated it. I also struggled in my classes, partly because they were hard and partly because I simply didn't care about electromagnetics, physics, or differential equations. Despite this, after what my dad said, I couldn't quit.

So I carried on.

As I've explained, the summer after my sophomore year, I worked for a high school mission's trip organization as a kids club coordinator responsible for running a crazy VBS-like ministry for local children between the ages of 5-15. That summer, I fell in love with kids and with ministry. I was more exhausted than I'd ever been before but also happier than I'd ever been, confident that I was doing exactly what God was calling me to do.

Up until that point, I'd made my career decision independent of my faith. While I'd considered how likely various majors would be to land me a good, well-paying job and whether or not they'd please my parents, it had never occurred to me to consider how following Jesus might impact my career choice.

My summer doing missions work changed that. After that, I started questioning God's will for my life and in particular, for my career. But at that point, I was halfway through one of the best engineering programs in the country, so it felt foolish to change direction.

So I continued on in electrical engineering, no longer hating it but certainly not loving it either.

Meanwhile, more and more of my friends began saying things like, "When I graduate, God is calling me to teach in the inner city... Or to do mission work in China... Or to work for a nonprofit organization."

I kept wondering, "How do you know what God is calling you to?"

In Scripture it seems so easy. Just look at Simon and Andrew. One day, they're working in the family business, fishing with their father, fairly content. The next, Jesus sees them and says, "Come, follow me, and I will make you fishers of men" (Matthew 4:19, ESV).

Boom. Just like that, Simon and Andrew drop their nets to go and do what God is calling them to do.

It seems so easy.

I mean, if Jesus had explicitly told me what to do with my life, I would gladly have done it.

But he didn't.

So I had to figure it out for myself.

My senior year, I led a girls' small group for my campus ministry. One night, we were talking about our plans for after graduation. I distinctly remember telling my friends, "I think God is calling me into youth ministry, but for that to happen, he's going to have to slam every other door shut in my face."

Turns out, that's exactly what he did.

I was rejected from job after job. By the time I graduated, I could have wallpapered my room with all the rejection letters I'd received from various places. As I lamented this to a friend and mentor, he said, "You know why that is, Jen. That's not what you're supposed to do. Why don't you try applying for some jobs in youth ministry?"

He pointed me towards a couple of websites, and I applied to a few different jobs. After a few interviews, I had a couple of job offers. Left with literally no other alternative, I reluctantly accepted one, all the while thinking, "I can always go back to electrical engineering."

I never did.

To be clear, it's not because everything was awesome as soon as I decided to follow God's call for my life.

It wasn't.

My first year in ministry, I commuted 40 miles each way to my job. The long commute was worth it because I loved my job... until things VERY rapidly fell apart and I was forced to leave, a little over a year after I began. When I did, I was emotionally bruised and battered, having been severely wounded by the church.

To make matters worse, that year my relationship with my parents was rough. They were understandably upset and confused by my decision to go into youth ministry—especially after they worked hard to pay for four years of college. I think they saw their investment as a waste. Knowing I'd deeply disappointed them broke my heart.

Choosing to go into youth ministry was a decision that I paid dearly for, in multiple ways. Yet it was absolutely the right one.

As a follower of Jesus, I couldn't ignore the fact that God was calling me into youth ministry—and not because it was ministry verses a "secular" job. Make no mistake: Ministry is NOT the only vocation that Jesus calls his followers to.

My husband actually uses his engineering degree. He and I both believe he's doing the work Jesus is calling him to.

Why?

Because he loves it, he's good at it, and it's needed. The same is true of youth ministry for me. I love it, I'm good at it—it uses every single gift God has given me—and it makes a difference in the lives of others.

As author Frederick Buechner says, "The place God calls you to is the place where your deep gladness and the world's deep hunger meet."

For my husband, that's software development. For me, that's youth ministry.

Where is it for you? Where does your deep gladness meet the world's deep hunger?

Wherever it is, do that.

Chances are good that unlike Simon and Andrew, Jesus is never audibly going to call you into a specific career path. But he is still inviting you to join in his Kingdom work of loving people—something you can do in any number of career paths. When you use your God-given gifts, regardless of whether you're making software, cleaning houses, or defending criminals, you're following Jesus and honoring God.

JESUS Talk

1. What do you want to be when you grow up? Do you think this is what God is calling you to do? Why or why not?
2. Answer Jen's question: "How do you know what God is calling you to do?"
3. Why's it important to understand that "ministry is NOT the only vocation that Jesus calls his followers to"?
4. According to author Frederick Buechner, "The place God calls you to is the place where your deep gladness and the world's deep hunger meet." Where does your deep gladness meet the world's deep hunger? How might realizing this help you determine your vocation?
5. What role can and should following Jesus play in determining your career? Why?

49: Don't Be Afraid

A few years ago, I had a major freak out.

My husband and I were backpacking in Arizona just outside the Grand Canyon. On our second day, we planned to hike from our base camp down to a lower waterfall. I'd read about this particular hike and knew that it contained several switchbacks—narrow paths up and down the side of a mountain or canyon—as well as a crude ladder chiseled into the canyon wall.

The night before, I'd laid awake, nervous about our descent. Then we began. I took maybe six steps before I made a crucial mistake.

I looked down.

As soon as I did, I became fearful—so fearful that I had a panic attack. I couldn't catch my breath. I frantically clung to the canyon wall convinced that if I moved even an inch, I would plummet to my death. I stood there, sobbing hysterically. Nothing my husband did or said could convince me to go on because in that moment, I tasted fear.

If I'm honest, that's not the only time I've tasted fear. There are actually lots of things I'm afraid of including ticks, mice, losing my job, and my husband and/or daughter dying.

I'm guessing there are also things you're afraid of.

Maybe you're afraid of heights or doctors or failing a test or a class. Maybe you're afraid your parents will get divorced or that you'll have to move. Perhaps you're afraid of leaving for college or of not getting into college. Maybe you're afraid of never figuring out what you're supposed to do with your life or perhaps you worry you'll never fall in love. Maybe like me, you fear death—your own or that of someone you love.

> "I have a fear of small, tangible things, like squirrels. Bigger fears exist as well. A recent big fear of mine was not getting into the college I wanted to go to. It was constantly on my mind. Through communion, as well as other reminders of Jesus's love, I started to realize that in Jesus, there is no room for fear. I still struggle to let go of my fears, but through Jesus's love I have started to accept that failure is okay, that I can't always fear the unknown, and that squirrels may not actually be so mean after all."
>
> — ELLIE

Like it or not, we all fear something.

No wonder then, that one of the phrases uttered most in Scripture is "Don't be afraid." Sometimes, it's an angel who says this. Other times, it's Jesus himself.

As followers of Jesus, we need not be afraid.

Now, as someone who's pretty much always been afraid of something, for a long time I simply ignored these words. I thought they applied to specific people in specific times and places. Now, I'm not so sure.

Maybe one of the differences Jesus makes in our lives is that we really, truly don't have to be afraid. I mean, as followers of Jesus,

241

what have we to fear?

As followers of Jesus, no matter how alone we feel, we are loved, deeply and perfectly by the one who knows us best: our Creator.

As followers of Jesus, even if we never find a fulfilling job, we still have a purpose: to join in God's Kingdom work.

As followers of Jesus, death cannot destroy us; Jesus already conquered it.

So as followers of Jesus, maybe we really, truly need not fear.

I'd like to believe that... Really, I would. But practically speaking, how do we stop fearing things?

I think Jesus' friend Peter shows us how.

Matthew tells the story of how one day, Jesus' friends are hanging out on a boat without him. Eventually, Jesus realizes he misses his friends so he decides to take a quick walk across the water in order to reach them.

It's the middle of the night, so when Jesus' friends look up and see him walking on water, they assume he's a ghost and freak out. Immediately, Jesus utters our favorite phrase: "Take courage! It is I. Don't be afraid."

As soon as he hears Jesus, Peter decides he's got to go to him. So he jumps out of the boat and starts walking on water.

He does fine for a while but then he gets distracted by the wind. He takes his eyes off Jesus and begins to sink. Immediately, he gets scared. Desperate, he cries out to Jesus, who reaches out, grabs his hand and catches him (Matthew 14:22-33).

I don't know about you, but I see a lot of myself in Peter. For a while, everything is fine. But then, just as I did that day in the canyon, I look down. I take my eyes off Jesus and start to sink. I grow fearful because I forget to remember that Jesus has got me, safe in his grasp.

> "Even when we are walking down a tunnel of darkness, we are walking with someone else and will always be guided in the right direction."
>
> — KIM

But, you see, that's the key. If you don't want to be afraid, there's only one thing you need to do: Remember Jesus.

Remember that you belong to Jesus.

Remember that you're safe in Jesus' grasp, that he's got you.

Remember that Jesus loves you.

Remember what Jesus did for you.

That sounds easy, right? Then why, oh why, is it so hard to actually do?

Because sometimes, we forget.

Maybe that's why one of the last things Jesus does with his friends is give them a reminder. On the night of his arrest, Jesus gathers his friends for a farewell dinner. He knows that in just a few short hours, he'll be arrested, beaten, and put to death and that his friends will live in fear that they will be too.

So Jesus breaks some bread and passes around some wine and tells them, "Do this in remembrance of me" (Luke 22:19-20).

Jesus knows that despite their best intentions, as soon as he's no longer with them, his friends will forget. So he gives them—and us—a tangible way to remember.

It's called communion.

The next time you take it, my prayer for you is this: May you remember that Jesus has already won, that you are his, that you are loved, and that as a result, you have nothing to fear.

JESUS Talk

1. What are you afraid of? Why?
2. Answer Jen's question, "As followers of Jesus, what have we to fear?"
3. What in your life causes you to forget Jesus?
4. How might taking communion help you to remember Jesus and as a result, make you less afraid?
5. Jen tells us to "Remember that you belong to Jesus. Remember that you're safe in Jesus' grasp; that he's got you. Remember that Jesus loves you. Remember what Jesus did for you." Today, which of these things do you most need to remember? Why?

"Today, I just felt like crying after my AP English class. On the way to chorus, I started crying. I looked down on my finger, and I saw this ring I just got. It has the little fishy on it. It was a God moment. I was reminded that Jesus is here for me. He's my rock. He's my strength. He's trying to say, 'It's going to be okay.'"

— SYDNEY

50: Don't Give Up

Near the end of his Gospel, Luke tells a bizarre story.

In it, two of Jesus' followers, Cleopas and his pal, are walking to a village called Emmaus. Along the way, they're talking about everything that's just happened, including the arrest, trial, and crucifixion of their leader, Jesus.

As they're talking, Jesus himself comes up and walks along with them but—and this is a big but—for some unknown reason, they're "kept from recognizing him."

Making conversation, Jesus asks, "What are you talking about?"

In response, Cleopas asks a question of his own, "Where have you been? How's it possible that you don't know what's been happening?"

Ignoring Cleopas' question, Jesus responds, "What's been happening?"

At this, Cleopas gives Jesus a crash course—the SparkNotes version—of the events of the last few days. He says, "We're talking about Jesus of Nazareth. He performed miracles, taught some crazy stuff, and forgave sins. He was a prophet, powerful in word and deed before God and all the people. The chief priests and our rulers handed him over to be sentenced to death, and they crucified him;

but we had hoped that he was the one who was going to redeem Israel."

Read that last sentence again.

"We *had* hoped that he was the one who was going to redeem Israel."

In other words, these guys—along with the rest of Jesus' followers— once believed he was the long-awaited Messiah, the one sent by God to save and free them. But they don't anymore. Their hope was crushed when they saw Jesus—the one they thought was going to redeem Israel—die on a cross.

Maybe you can relate. Like these early followers of Jesus, maybe you've also had your hopes crushed. Like them, maybe you've uttered a similar phrase, "I had hoped...

> ... that I'd get a date to homecoming."
> ... that I'd get into my number one choice of colleges."
> ... that I'd get a scholarship for school."
> ... that Dad would find another job."
> ... that Mom and Dad would stop fighting."
> ... that Grandma's cancer would be healed."

I, too, have experienced the devastation that comes with having your dreams crushed. For me, that sentence goes like this, "I had hoped to have a child."

I even thought I was going to. Two years ago, I took a pregnancy test on a Tuesday morning and when it came back positive, my husband and I rejoiced. But less than a week later, I started bleeding.

We lost our baby in the miscarriage I mentioned earlier.

It was horrible. One moment, we had everything we wanted. The next, it felt like our world was ending.

I imagine that's how Cleopas and his friend felt as they walked to Emmaus.

"We had hoped..."

But now they have no hope. Nevertheless, they tell Jesus more about the events of the last few days.

"And what is more, it is the third day since all this took place"—a significant day since on more than one occasion Jesus had suggested something spectacular would happen on that day.

Cleopas goes on to say, "Some of our women amazed us. They went to the tomb early this morning but didn't find his body. They came and told us they had seen a vision of angels who said he was alive. Then some of our companions went to the tomb and found it just as the women had said, but him they did not see."

Umm, guys? Why can't you connect the dots? The one you had hoped would redeem you said he'd rise on the third day. Then on the third day, when your friends find an empty tomb you're suddenly confused?

"Jesus is someone who helps you through tough times and is there for you, even if no one else is."

— JJ

Indeed, they are.

So Jesus explains Scripture to them.

All of it.

Bit by bit, Jesus points out everything Scripture says about him.

Eventually, the threesome arrive in Emmaus and Cleopas invites

Jesus to stay with them. He agrees and that night, they eat dinner together. Jesus takes bread, give thanks, breaks it, and gives it to them. When he does, their eyes are opened and they recognize him who has been with them all along (Luke 24:13-35).

Long before Jesus' followers had reason to hope, they put their trust in him, their faith in him.

In the depths of their despair following Jesus' crucifixion—in the eternity that was Holy Saturday, the day Jesus remained in the tomb—they felt their hope dissipate.

But then, on Easter, they discover that the one in whom they'd begun to hope is in fact their reason for hope.

At the table in Emmaus, Jesus restores their hope. In fact, Jesus becomes their hope.

The same is true for us.

Jesus is our hope. He's the reason why, in the face of crushing disappointment and suffering, we can go on.

What Jesus' resurrection teaches us is that life comes from death.

It may not always feel like it.

> "Jesus gave us hope and an understanding of what it means to be children of God."
> — ERIC

Believe me. I know.

In the days following the loss of my child, I wanted nothing more than to crawl up in a ball and sob. (And for a while, I did.) But there, curled up in the fetal position, I encountered Jesus—as real as he's ever been to me. In him, I found reason to hope.

That's the difference Jesus makes in our lives.

Now, to clarify, our hope in Jesus is different than optimism.

Optimism says that when we don't get what we want, we'll make the best of our situation. It says that in the face of suffering, if we can just put on a happy face, life will eventually get better.

Hope says something much different than that.

Hope acknowledges we may never get what we want. It admits our suffering might continue. Hope is believing that no matter what our circumstances, God is at work. For this reason, hope can be found even in the midst of our greatest despair, even when we feel nothing but sad. Hope is not merely putting on a happy face. Hope is trusting in God's promises because, like Cleopas and his friend, we've seen that through Jesus' death and resurrection, we have every reason to.

Hope is not a magic superpower. It doesn't fix everything... but it does enable us to survive.

Without Jesus, there is no hope. Without Jesus, we'd only ever be able to say, "We *had* hoped..."

But thanks to Jesus' death and resurrection, we no longer need to utter those words.

Instead we can confidently say, "We have hope," because Jesus *is* hope.

JESUS Talk

1. How would you complete this sentence: "I had hoped..."? In other words, when have your hopes been crushed? What was that experience like for you?
2. According to Jen, "Jesus is our hope. He's the reason why, in the face of crushing disappointment and suffering, we can go on." In the face of crushing disappointment or suffering, how has Jesus helped you go on?
3. "What Jesus' resurrection teaches us is that life comes from death." What evidence of this have you seen in your life?
4. What's the difference between hope and optimism?
5. "Hope is trusting in God's promises because we've seen that through Jesus' death and resurrection, we have every reason to." What are the promises of God that you need to trust in right now? Why?
6. To you, what does it mean that "Jesus is hope"?

Acknowledgments

Thanks to those who have made this book possible:

The good folks at the Youth Cartel, for your willingness to do crazy things like publish a theology book disguised as a devotional for teens;

Those who, throughout the years, have helped me fall more deeply in love with Jesus (you know who you are);

The Palatine Misfits for giving me a safe place to doubt and for teaching me that life is meant to be lived together;

FLY's adult leaders, for faithfully manifesting Jesus to our teens (and to me);

The 2014-2015 and 2015-2016 FLY Student Leadership Team for reading early chapters of this devotional and helping me to create a book that teens will actually enjoy;

Rebecca and Melanie, for reading every word of this book and showing me how to make it better;

Doug, for embodying Jesus to me and reminding me that HE is what truly matters.